A Ship Without An Udder

ROBERT L. STEED

Illustrations by Jack Davis

LONGSTREET PRESS
Atlanta, Georgia

Published by
LONGSTREET PRESS, INC.
A subsidiary of Cox Newspapers,
A division of Cox Enterprises, Inc.
2140 Newmarket Parkway
Suite 118
Marietta, GA 30067

Printed in the United States

1st Printing 1995

Library of Congress Catalog Card Number 95-77252

ISBN 1-56352-252-7

Book design and typesetting by Jill Dible
Cover Illustration by Jack Davis

Electronic film prep and separations by Advertising Technologies, Inc., Atlanta, GA

To Lu. You're still the One.

—RLS

OTHER STEED BOOKS,
THE MOVIE RIGHTS TO WHICH ARE STILL AVAILABLE,

Willard Lives!

Lucid Intervals

Money, Power and Sex (A Self-Help Guide for All Ages)

The Sass Menagerie

Mail Fraud: The Laughable Letters of Robert L. Steed

Contents

Mr. Claude (Just Call Me "Chuck") Perry
Maximum Publisher
Longstreet Press
2140 Newmarket Parkway, Suite 118
Marietta, GA 30067

Re: *Title of Opus No. 6*

Dear Claude:

Regarding our periodic and ever nettlesome quandary as to what to name one of my collections of bilious nonsense, I believe that fate, in the unlikely form of my wiry wife, has come up with a title that will pique the interest of prospective readers from sea to shining sea. As you well know, she continues without surcease her unremitting cavalcade of malapropisms, mangled and mixed metaphors, crushed clichés, gut-shot similes, and generally weird utterances. They are spawned with a degree of unremitting energy and frequency which defies calm description.

To digress a bit and offer just a few mind-numbing recent examples, I would repeat a colloquy which took place between Lu and our daughter Georgia, who, having spotted a biography of Harriet Beecher Stowe on Lu's night table asked, "What is this Harriet Beecher Stowe?" Whereupon, Lu, in a very arch manner befitting someone who reads the *New York Times* (mostly to me while I am trying to read the local paper), said, "Well, you know she's the one who wrote *Little Tom's Cabin*." Georgia turned to me rolling her eyes and said, "I don't think she's gotten very far in the book."

On another occasion, while discussing the estate of a deceased friend, Lu said, "That widow just rushed in and commandereared the whole thing," evoking images of painful times in the probate court. She also confided to me that she was "well seeped in art" and, on another subject, that a hapless friend had "moved from the fat to the fire" (apparently without the benefit of any frying pan).

More recently, after a local TV crew had come by to interview us on camera about how we had managed to stay together for so long ("Codger marriages; film at 11:00"), Lu, having observed me resting my jaw on my hand during the taping in a futile attempt to obscure a dangling wattle, accused me of being "furgative." When I inquired as to precisely what she meant by that term, she said, "I saw you over there holding your chin and pontiferating."

But swinging back to business at hand, a catchy (read "cunningly commercial") title for the book, I was encouraged some months ago when I heard Lu say to a glassy-eyed listener that something was "as useless as tits on a tombstone." Frankly, I was intrigued by the poetic imagery involved (not to mention my eternal fascination as to what sort of blown circuitry in her medulla oblongata would provoke such an utterance), and thought she might have unwittingly given us a good title.

On reflection, however, I decided that naming the book "As Useless as Tits on a Tombstone," might cost us our hoped for PG rating, and that inclusion of the word "useless" in the title cut too close to the bone in terms of suggesting to prospective readers the real literary value of the collection itself.

Happily, I didn't have to wait long for my sinewy spouse to serve up another possibility. We were at Chastain Park when I heard her fervently discussing with one of our guests the sad loss by my *alma mater*, Mercer, of one of its key employees. Lu said breathlessly that, "When that woman left for another college, Mercer was like a ship without an udder." In a transcendent moment of blinding clarity I realized we had our title—*A Ship Without an Udder!*

The only thing that now remains to be done is to see if we can cajole Jack Davis into illustrating yet another of these dubious enterprises and assay how many copies we can inflict on an unsuspecting reading public. Given your guile and cunning (I am speaking now of your personality traits and not the fly-by-night law firm of the same name you use to negotiate your book contracts with trusting but naive authors), I know that we will have a best-seller on our hands if not our consciences.

With every good wish to you and all under your protection, I am

Increasingly incontinent

Robert L. Steed

A Modest Proposal: Humor Impaired? Try Rule 5

In the summer of 1978, the editor of the *Atlanta Journal-Constitution* was a spindle-shanked character named Hal Gulliver. Gulliver was lured into the newspaper business after winning an H. L. Mencken look-alike contest which was easy enough for him as he wore his hair slicked down with Brilliantine, affected rumpled suits and suspenders; smoked cheap, noisome cigars; and had a pair of ears that could have been used on a 1950 Buick Roadmaster as curb feelers. (In late 1987, Gulliver, who had by then left the newspaper business to become a lawyer, pushed away from the supper table, belched robustly and said to his wife, "I'm going to drive over to the Winn-Dixie and get me some of them Milk Duds." He was never seen again.)

For reasons known only to editor Gulliver, he thought I should begin writing a humor column on the op-ed pages of the *Constitution* and suggested that I become a contributor on a regular basis.

My day job in the ever-exciting world of municipal finance law would not permit any effort involving daily or even weekly deadlines but I did, at his urging, become a dilettante columnist and have contributed sassy essays of dubious literary merit to the pages of the *Atlanta Journal-Constitution* since that happy encounter.

Over the intervening seventeen years, I have been perpetually baffled, amazed, and sometimes terrified to observe just how literally readers can take something which is at best an attempt at humor and at worst pure nonsense. Their grave and stormy reactions to the froth I have offered up is truly astounding, and in a rare contemplative moment, usually brought on by a couple of Irish whiskeys, I will ponder the nagging question as to just how, when, and why our society became so dreadfully humor impaired.

A real columnist, Russell Baker, recently said, "The land is swarming with people willing to spend their lives being offended, whether the offender is offensive or not." I couldn't agree more. Based on clinical data gathered over my mediocre career as a part-time columnist, I have learned that there is no statement too silly or shallow as to avoid causing the underwear on some overserious reader to bunch up.

We are in the grip of a horrendous wave of debilitating political correctness, and it may take our spirit under if the seas of the easily outraged don't soon subside.

There seem to be no safe subjects for humor which do not provoke some eye-bugging outraged response.

To give just a few examples in support of my slender premise, I would point to a column I wrote some years back in which I said I thought *Swan Lake* would draw bigger crowds if it had more tap dancing. An innocent enough bit of nonsense, one would think, but it provoked someone with the Atlanta Symphony Orchestra to send an invective-dripping letter to the editor saying it was no wonder that folks up north thought the South was a cultural Sahara if a major newspaper like the

Constitution would allow some fool like me to write some foolishness like that.

In another column I revealed that cigars were originally invented as breath fresheners for people who eat dead birds. I received a telephone call from an outraged lawyer in middle Georgia who had gone to the trouble to look up my number so he could call me to say he was sure that wasn't true.

I wrote a column offering helpful tidbits from my treasure trove of marital advice and, in the process, suggested to young husbands that it was better not to ask your wife if her hose were wrinkled unless you were absolutely sure she was wearing hose.

This bit of innocent insolence so provoked the militant feminists (and there may be something of a redundancy in the term) that they fell into a hysterical gang rant, writing angry letters to the editor with the relentlessness of tracer bullets.

You would be frightened at the angry reaction I got from the religious right when I suggested in an early column on the Right Rev. Jim Bakker that he looked like an ordained chipmunk and that his then-wife, the bountiful Tammy Faye, looked like a makeup consultant for Zayres. I say *you* would be frightened. I was so frightened that I had my wife start my car for almost three months. (Subsequently, Rev. Jim Bakker had his zip code changed by federal authorities and the ever-lachrymose Tammy Faye was voluntarily admitted to the Betty Ford Clinic for Maybelline Abuse.)

Having observed all of this clinical material over the years, I have become something of an expert in categorizing humor-impaired groups as to which has the least sense of humor. In the pantheon of the overly grave there are a lot of obvious groups that come to mind—lawyers and doctors certainly take themselves awfully seriously from time to time. Doctors' wives also take it very seriously if one writes anything critical about their demigod doctors, such as (to cite an unhappy example in one of my columns), "I know a doctor who defines unnecessary surgery as performing an operation when you don't even need the money." This brought forth a number of letters from angry doctors' wives who wrote in grueling detail just how their husbands had struggled through and been rendered impecunious by colleges, medical schools, extended and impoverished residencies, and were thus damn well entitled to collect Krugerrands, drive outrageously expensive foreign cars, and make dopey real estate investments. I have to confess that their indignant replies never failed to cause a tear to run down my ample cheeks.

Baptists, of which I am one, often take themselves too seriously, as do physical fitness buffs, folks who clog the public streets on those spindly bicycles with seats the size of a club face on a three iron, politicians, preachers, environmentalists, deer hunters, NRA members, the dueling Jesses—Jackson (I'm never sure just how he earns his living) and Helms (who perpetually undercuts any notion that North Carolina residents harbor progressive thoughts). People just seem so eager to declare themselves victims and set up an angry whine.

If I were forced at gunpoint to choose which group is the most humor impaired (happily, that is a remote possibility as those gaining access to our chambers must pass through a metal detector and, depending on how randy the receptionist is, are often subject to rigorous frisking as well), I would have to say that the militant feminists are the most eager to take offense whether, as Russell Baker says, the offender is offensive or not. With almost no provocation they can be offended to the brink of incontinence.

I'm always amazed when the militant feminists find fault with my work product. I am so widely known as being supersensitive to the feminist agenda that Alan Alda and Phil Donahue will often call on me for advice as to how they might be more in tune with the times. (I have advised them both that, short of cross-dressing, I don't think they can do much more than they're doing now.)

Moreover, I will often challenge male chauvinists with the question, "How would you like to wake up one morning and realize that every day for the rest of your lives you would have to shave your legs and dance backwards?" Just reflecting on my query has caused many of them to become more sensitive and to adopt more progressive behavior patterns, i.e. crying in front of their spouses, trying for more honest communication, and not leaving the toilet seat up.

However, despite my unblemished record in this regard, the steaming sisters are forever taking umbrage at my observations (and, if you've never seen a militant feminist taking umbrage, I should warn you, it's not a pretty sight).

They are particularly hard on me when I make any mention of my wizened wife of many years. Such references provoke cries of flared-nostril outrage on the part of the easily offended harridans who will inundate me and my editors with howls of incensed anguish. They claim that I say rude or insensitive things about my sinewy spouse though nothing could be further from the truth. I avoid doing so for several reasons. First, she's mean as a snake—vicious, cunning, and cruel—and second, as any husband with half a grain of sense knows, there comes a time during every twenty-four-hour span when you are going to be in bed asleep while your wife is still up stalking about. And, if you have said anything rude or insensitive to her, she can take that unhappy moment to grab some blunt (or worse yet, sharp) instrument and do you grievous bodily harm. We all knew that *Bobbitt* was a last name but only recently did we learn its dreadful implications as a verb.

What, anxious and inquiring minds want to know, can be done about this growing hole in our humor ozone?

My solution to this humor-impaired malaise in which we find ourselves wallowing is to take heed of the classic admonition offered by Rule 5 of the Kansas General Assembly. It is said that around the turn of the century the Kansas legislature offered several rules of great weight and merit and only number 5 has survived the intervening years. I believe it survives because it is a paradigm of good common sense. It goes (and this is the way they wrote it), "Don't take yourself so damn serious."

I believe that is a marvelous maxim to live by and commend it to every man jack of you (women jacks too if we didn't lose them in the foregoing ramble on militant feminists).

I don't believe the Kansas solons meant to say that we should not take our relationships or responsibilities seriously. Rather, I think they meant that we should put some distance between ourselves and our own points of view lest those points of view become too rigid, intractable, and unyielding. As Ralph Waldo Emerson (it was either Ralph Waldo Emerson or Merv Griffin; I'm always getting those two mixed up) once said, "It is virtually impossible to overestimate the unimportance of most things."

It was in that spirit that the following bits of frivolous flotsam and jetsam were hatched and uttered.

Keep Rule 5 in mind. Don't take yourself so damn serious.

—RLS

A Prince of a Guy?

If all those letters to *Penthouse* were set to music, what you would have is a Prince concert. If you crossed Robin Hood in purple tights with a lookout for a massage parlor, what you'd have is Prince himself.

For reasons that I can't recall and perhaps never fully understood, I went to the Omni with my aging rock 'n' roll wife to see and painfully hear the vaunted Love Sexy World (No Cameras) Tour '88 featuring Prince (no last name). I must admit that on one level I was a willing participant. After hearing so much about him, I was more than a little curious as to why a rock singer who was apparently named after a dog and who looked like an anorexic Little Richard was the subject of so much attention and adulation. I came away with ringing ears but otherwise unenlightened.

After a carnal and noisy two and one-half hours, I determined that Mr. Prince, a native of Minneapolis (one of the first

PRINCE
JACK DAVIS

places you'd think to go if you were looking for a sex symbol), is one of those folks who give vulgarity a bad name.

Performing in the round before a packed and enthusiastic house, the Prince pranced in five-inch heels (as far as I could tell he was not wearing pantyhose) and walked a line between lubricity and spirituality or, as he himself put it so eloquently, "It's easy to be nasty; what's hard is being perfect in the eyes of God." This breathtakingly trenchant truth was piously uttered after an hour of song and dance so nasty as to bring a blush to the sallow cheeks of Dr. Ruth. But, again using the *Penthouse* metaphor, each issue apparently needs a socially redeeming insert to stay just shy of crossing the pornographic point of no return, thus avoiding possible criminal prosecution. Where is Hinson McAuliff when we really need him?

Prince's shift from the salaciously secular to the spiritual realm consisted of a few gratuitous gospel numbers such as "It Is No Secret What God Can Do" and "I Wish You Heaven," bringing to my mind the eternal verity in the old black spiritual "Everybody Talking 'Bout Heaven Ain't Going There." All of this pseudosanctimonious stuff was interspersed with coital pantomime which would make the casual observer think that some Broadway impresario had assayed to set a sex manual to music. These maneuvers for the most part were performed by Prince and three lascivious ladies wearing what appeared to be orthopedic black garter belts from Frederick's of Smyrna. One of the trio was so beefy she looked like Tina Turner on steroids.

The entire concupiscent concert was accompanied by so much special lighting and so many speakers that the lights in the metro area must have dimmed when the concert cranked up.

If the Prince is interested in my opinion (and you'd be surprised at how many rock stars slip into my chambers from time to time seeking counsel), I would tell him that what his program needs is some punctuation. There is absolutely no way the unschooled ear can determine when one song ends and the other begins. I thought the first half of the show was just one long tune with a variety of prurient prancing. Actually, I learned later that there were probably eight or nine different tunes involved but only the *cognoscenti* can tell where one stops and the other starts.

All of this business is performed in more billowing smoke and purple gas than a large pulp mill could generate. I hope the promoters were required to file an environmental impact study before staging the concert.

It was a memorable show and worth attending just for the crowd reaction but, after taking in Prince, I don't think today's raunchy royalty is any match for the musical monarchs of the past—say Count Basie or Duke Ellington.

October 20, 1988

To Thine Own Scalp Be True

All this political mendacity oozing through television tubes into our living rooms (or, in the case of Democrats, dens) is having an unhealthy effect on advertising in general.

It seems clear to me that if advertisers are even partially successful in palming off George Bush as a Texan or Michael Dukakis as a moderate, who knows what lengths they will go to in future attempts to euchre the American public.

Ever alert to any attempt to lower the nation's gullibility threshold, I have been scanning the cable television channels for any distant early warnings that advertisers are seeking commercial advantages which might be bobbing about in this sea of false impressions set adrift by political image makers. (I don't know about you, but these nautical metaphors are making me queasy.)

The other evening as I was watching one of those double-digit cable channels in the upper reaches of cable TV, there appeared a commercial which made me think that the men in the gray flannel suits were convinced that the nation's collective credulity had been completely sapped by the outrageous claims of the presidential aspirants. The specific commercial that concerned me so promised a surefire way for hapless balding men to re-fuzz their glabrous domes, but in a way so cunning as to assure that even their closest friends and business associates would never be aware of the reforestation.

The spot opens with a handsome, albeit hairless, young business type bopping around an office with a briefcase while an attractive receptionist barely gives him the time of day. The promoters of the process, which, according to the ad, is a "non-surgical hair progression," promise to restore hair so subtly and gradually that even close business associates and friends will never suspect what's afoot or, in this case, ahead.

During a one-minute commercial, the hero of the spot goes from being so bald that he has to carry his dandruff in his watch pocket to being so hairy that he looks like a pair of Lhasa apsos are mating on his noggin. I'm not kidding—the guy goes from Mr. Clean to Wolfman Jack in just a few weeks and *nobody* notices except, of course, the attractive receptionist who begins to gaze at him so rapturously it appears she's having a glandular meltdown.

My point is—and I bet you thought we'd never get to it—What's wrong with electing a scion of inherited wealth from Connecticut or a liberal dwarf to the presidency? What's wrong with being bald? Why can't folks be happy with themselves and others as they really are? Just as an aside, I think the foregoing questions put the lie to the oft-uttered statement that there are no deep thinkers around these days.

Some may think this sensitive exposition is nothing more than a crass promotion of my new book on baldness, *Hairless and Happy in Our Time* (Simon & Lipshutz, New York, Philadelphia and Austell), but the truth is that I think folks should accept themselves and others for what they are.

As to baldness, I think men look a lot better with no hair than wearing some sorry looking rug that looks as though it were made from a bad piece of Astroturf. Burt Reynolds looked very macho in *Deliverance* but since then has succumbed to a succession of hairpieces, each looking sillier than the one before it. Willard Scott just can't seem to decide on his top dressing. One day his head will be as clean as a houndstooth, and the next day he shows up with, get this, a balding hairpiece. (Researchers at the University of Georgia School of Veterinary Medicine revealed in a recent study that a houndstooth really isn't all that clean, but until the National Center for Clichés and Similes comes up with a reasonable alternative, I plan to stick with something with a proven record.) I happen to think that Joe Garagiola and Sean Connery are good-looking, manly folks. As my friend, Mac Teate, a quality control inspector for Bowdon, Georgia's Annual Bull Chip Derby, boasts to his friends about his clean-cut brow, "This is a solar collector for a finely tuned sex machine." It should be noted that his wife said, "Mac's not getting enough sun." But my point is that bald men should hold their heads high (except, of course, on real sunny days when glare becomes a problem).

All of this is to say that if the image makers don't stop greasing the skids so egregiously, I think I may abandon both candidates. If Willard Scott could ever make up his mind, I might go for him as a write-in.

November 4, 1988

Flogging a Book to Death

As I sat in the green room of a local television station awaiting an opportunity to go on the air to flog my latest book, (*The Sass Menagerie*, $14.95 hardback, available at fine bookstores everywhere or, for orders of two or more, I'll come out to your house, apartment, or double-wide and sign anything in that sucker you want or, if you choose, autograph articles of intimate apparel), it occurred to me that there must be a better way to spur book sales than this approach. I was even more firmly convinced when I only had a two-minute sliver of time and was followed by a ferret from the Atlanta Zoo who got five minutes even though he couldn't talk. When I testily made this observation to the anchorman after the show, he said, "That's why the ferret got more time."

Driving back to the office from the interview, a sudden surge of blood reached my brain and the ultimate solution to hyping book sales occurred to me with blinding clarity. That is, of course, to get the Ayatollah Khomeini to condemn publicly the book and threaten my life or, preferably, the lives of my publishers, Simon & Lipschutz (New York, Philadelphia and Austell). Why hadn't I thought of that in the first place?

When the Great One, in his role as Exalted Literary Critic, hurled bans at the recently published *Satanic Verses* by Salman Rushdie, sales went off the charts. There was, of course, a dark side to the publicity in that the Ayatollah offered $5,200,000 to anyone who would send Rushdie to that great Autograph Party in the Sky. I confess right up front that I would be a little intimidated about this aspect of the program but, for a real rush in book sales, I would be willing to have my wife start my car every morning for a year or so.

Attempting to put that pale thought to vivid action, I called long-distance information and attempted to get the telephone number of the Ayatollah. Unfortunately, he has an unlisted tent and could not be reached. It was probably just as well because, searching my brain for anything in my last collection that might have the happy effect of giving offense to the Most Worthy One, I could only recall one blurb from a distant column to the effect that every time I saw him on television I thought it was Gabby Hayes in drag. Realizing deep down that this flip and off-the-cuff observation wouldn't generate an Iranian bounty of more than two or three hundred dollars, I began my quest for a condemnation by some other potentially indignant past victim of my venomous pen.

I called Roger Sund, the executive director of the Cobb County Chamber of Commerce, and pointed out that in one essay I had alleged that Cobb County was not as sophisticated as it held itself out to be, going on to report that a group of anthropologists at the University of Georgia had recently discovered a tribe of people living in the woods in south Cobb County who still worship the Big Chicken. I suggested to him that the Cobb chamber might want to put out a contract on me and offered to kick in a couple of hundred bucks to the fund myself if he could get some radio and TV time to publicize the threat. Sund said that he was not interested in that the chamber had already relocated all the Big Chicken worshipers in mobile homes near Smyrna and, "besides," he said, "nobody in Cobb County reads your stuff anyway."

Undaunted, I resumed poring over my prior literary output for other serious slights which could be thumped into a newsworthy public grievance with resulting salutary effects on book sales.

I had observed irreverently in the past that if Ronald Reagan had one more face-lift, his navel was going to pop up over his shirt collar but, on reflection, I decided a death threat from an ex-president would not even be sufficiently newsworthy to get a blurb in the classified section. I then recalled that I had once publicly suggested that Six Flags Over Georgia install a new thriller and death-defying attraction consisting of an automobile ride with Hosea Williams (talk about your Scream Machine). Remembering that Hosea was pretty volatile and, according to recent newspaper accounts, armed to the teeth, I called his office to see if he might utter a threat with respect to my book but through his secretary was given a polite brush-off to the following effect, "Tell that chump I ain't studying him."

If any readers have any suggestions as to how I might have given or could in the future give ultimate offense to some powerful and newsworthy person and provoke a public jihad along the line of the *Satanic Verses* hurrah in the process, I would welcome their suggestions. In the meantime, I am optimistically storing provisions in a secret hiding place (all I can tell you is that it is somewhere in the metro area) against the possibility that I might have to go underground for a spell if I ever come up with the right person to antagonize.

February 22, 1989

He Gives Good Jovi

Ever the unwitting and bumbling victim of cruel circumstance, I found myself on a recent evening at the Omni in a boiling mass of barely postpubescents attending a raucous concert performed by the oddly named Bon Jovi. An unhappy combination of gullibility and inattentiveness always causes me to be the constant dupe of my wiry wife's mercurial musical tastes.

In fact, through lack of attention on my part to her capricious planning and invitation accepting, I had gone from Scylla to Charybdis in the Omni in a span of just four days, having been a casualty of a Hank Williams Jr. concert on Saturday and the Bon Jovi musical mayhem the following Wednesday.

Correctly judging that reflections on "Why me Lord?" would not help me get through the musical ordeal which lay ahead, I busied myself comparing the crowd in which we had found ourselves engulfed the previous Saturday evening with Wednesday evening's wall-to-wall gaggle.

The contrast was startling. The crowd at the Hank Williams Jr. concert looked like a casting call for the love scene from *Deliverance*. They were a flint-eyed, beefy, and grizzled herd bedecked in camouflage outfits and Confederate memorabilia. The Bon Jovi aficionados, on the other hand, were an appealing, very young, well-scrubbed lot, heavy into miniskirts which looked to have been applied with paintbrushes or jeans which were so amply stuffed they looked as though they had been jumped into from a high place. Their general appearance was remarkably attractive save for the occasional young male whose ear sported an earring. I longed to point out to each of them that Willie Nelson never had a hit record after he had his ears pierced but sensed that my message would fall on deaf lobes.

Except for two suspicious-looking taxpayers in their forties with fedoras, shades, and dark suits who were apparently doing a bad Blues Brothers impression, I was the only gray-haired, neck-tied music lover in the place. In fact, as I came through the turnstile, a middle-aged ticket taker cracked at me, "You heard Guy Lombardo was dead, didn't you, Bud? It was in all the papers."

As is always the case, we were treated to a warm up act which, in this case, consisted of four anorexic and gratuitously bellicose teenagers aptly named Skid Row. Their routine, which looked like the Bataan Death March set to music, featured an endless amount of incomprehensible caterwauling.

They all wore tattered blue jeans and shoulder-length hair and looked like the children that Don Knotts refuses to discuss. Their upper arms were so spiderlike that the tattoos affected by some of them could only have been accomplished with microscopes.

Between their mind-numbing musical selections, they offered in language so foul that it would make Richard Pryor blanch, a philosophy for teenagers roughly as follows: "If like your boss, or your parents, like, or your teacher, like gets on your case and tells you what to do, well then, like, just tell them to go [expletive phrase suggesting an anatomically impossible sex act deleted] themselves. Because, like, man, that's what rock 'n' roll is all about." "Well," I huffed to my zoned out spouse, "I don't remember Pat Boone saying that's what rock 'n' roll was all about." Unfortunately, she cannot read lips and my protest was completely lost in the ongoing cacophony.

At length, Skid Row's barrage of trashy talk and death-defying decibels abated, and we were treated to the obligatory forty-five-minute wait while the stage was reset for the featured attraction. I can never understand why so much time and attention is given to this intermezzo in that all that is required in the way of instrumentation are extension cords and wall sockets.

During this interval the Bon Jovi roadies did what is benignly called a "sound check" with recorded music. As best I can tell, this consists of nothing more than turning up the volume on the tractor-trailer-size speakers to ensure that the street lights dim as far as Marietta and that everyone in the first twenty rows of the Omni is bleeding steadily from the nose and ears.

Amid fireworks and blinding light, Bon Jovi suddenly materialized onstage. Except for their keyboard pummeler who looked like the illicit love child of Phyllis Diller and the Phantom of the Opera, they were a far better-looking bunch than Skid Row. Curiously, all of their T-shirts, posters, and record albums featured the words "New Jersey" in letters of equal size and prominence following "Bon Jovi." I have known many people from New Jersey but none who would admit it so readily. It is a well-documented fact that when the Playboy Clubs opened in New Jersey, the bunnies dressed in rat suits. Printed on New Jersey license plates is the state motto: "What died?"

Though I had not heard any of their selections previously, I must confess that on balance their concert was a very entertaining and lively display. And, at times, their back beat got so basic that my toe began to tap involuntarily, causing the children in my vicinity to roll their eyes at me and gape as though Dame Margaret Rutherford had suddenly broken into a buck and wing.

As my grizzled spouse and I pulled the cotton from our ears

and joined the sated crowd lowing toward the exits, it occurred to me that I still didn't know if Bon Jovi was the name of the lead singer or the name of the group. When I ventured to ask, my wife, who is so old that when she went to college foreign language was still a required course, said tersely, "'Bon Jovi' is French for 'good Jovi.'" That was when I put the cotton back in my ears.

March 3, 1989

Wapner's World

I hate to sound like one of the old codgers sitting around some cafeteria or Howard Johnson's after gumming down another meal who, with a fresh squirt of blood to the brain, will start ruminating about "What is the world coming to?" However, having filed that disclaimer, I must admit to some disquiet when I read in the newspapers that in a recent poll more Americans recognized Judge Wapner of TV's *The People's Court* than any justice of the United States Supreme Court. Even more shocking, many could not name a single justice on the U.S. Supreme Court.

By the sheerest of coincidences, just a few days after my sluggish consciousness had been further numbed by this appalling intelligence, I was invited by a friend at WSB, the lively and zaftig Anna Ornduff, to have lunch with the good Judge Wapner, who was coming to town to flog his ultrasuccessful television program. Notwithstanding the fact that the name of

the program had always sounded to me like some communist Star Chamber, it is a phenomenon of the first order having been featured on the front page of the *Wall Street Journal*, in the *New Yorker*, on *20/20*, and in almost every major newspaper in the western world.

As I was keen to meet Judge Wapner in person, I accepted the WSB offer with alacrity (unfortunately, Alacrity had a conflicting engagement and couldn't make it to lunch with hizzoner, settling out of court for an autographed napkin).

The chief reason for my acute interest in meeting Wapner was to investigate a suspicion I had long harbored that the judge was really Ted Mack of the old *Original Amateur Hour*, who mysteriously disappeared in the early 1960s when television executives belatedly concluded that the American public was growing weary of C.P.A.s playing "The Flight of the Bumble-Bee" on a bicycle pump. When I first saw *The People's Court* I was convinced that the producers had recycled the benign and nasal Mack into a small-claims judge for purposes of television.

At our luncheon the good-natured Wapner responded without rancor to my gimlet-eyed inquiry by disclaiming any relation to Mack and produced a California driver's license and discharge papers to support his denial.

Thus assuaged, I dived into my City Grill lobster-and-corn chowder and resumed my furtive sidelong glances at Ms. Ornduff's impressive *balcon*, while thoroughly enjoying my visit with the handsome and genial Judge Joseph A. Wapner. I learned he was a real jurist who, in a pre-TV incarnation, served as presiding judge of the Los Angeles Superior Court, the largest court in the United States. The judge and his lively and lovely wife of forty-two years, Mickey, were so charming that I even resolved that if I assayed to write about him I would forswear any rude or flip comment like comparisons to Ted Mack of the *Original Amateur Hour*.

I also vowed to begin watching his program (which airs in

Atlanta at 5:30 P.M. on weekdays on Channel 2) and, having put that pale thought to vivid action a couple of evenings in a row, found it to be thoroughly enjoyable as the earnest, stern, and sometimes peckish Judge Wapner dispensed small-claims justice in a fair but summary fashion.

A typical case, titled "Bye Bye Basketballs," dealt with a backyard brouhaha involving two steaming litigants who barely spoke English. The plaintiff, a gnomish woman of middle years and uncertain national origin, was suing to recover three basketballs which her son had accidentally caused to land in the yard of a horribly truculent neighbor who heatedly explained to Judge Wapner in what I took to be an obscure Serbo-Croatian dialect why she refused to return them—"I'm sick wid dis beesketboll. I had flu wid fever and got so nervous I had to go for my stomach to de doctor."

The judge, with Solomon-like wisdom, ordered the basketballs returned and adjured the parties to work out their differences, pointing out to the flared-nostril and nettled neighbor that it was easier to give back the balls than to come to court at frequent intervals. She seemed unrepentant to me, and I suspect that her yard remains a Bermuda Triangle for errant basketballs notwithstanding the judge's wise and earnest counsel.

An interesting and regular postverdict feature of each show is a debriefing of the litigants by a prissy-looking court hanger-on named Doug Llewelyn. His interviews give the winners a chance to make sanctimonious noises about vindication while the losers' noses are rubbed in it with questions reminiscent of the famous "Aside from that, Mrs. Lincoln, how did you enjoy the play?" From all appearances, Llewelyn then disappears offstage to suck lemons and tease his hair.

This brings us back (and, you must be thinking, not a moment too soon) to what steps can be taken by the U.S. Supreme Court to enhance its lackluster public image. My suggestion is that the justices could reconsider their ban on televised arguments or they could urge President Bush to nominate Judge Wapner for the next seat which becomes vacant. Even if he doesn't get confirmed, it would give the FBI a chance to clear up those Ted Mack rumors once and for all.

July 11, 1989

Women of the World, Unite!

Self-introspection is often a painful process and, I must confess, it gives me more than a little chagrin to admit that in the past I have not been as sensitive to every aspect of the feminist movement as I might have been.

For the past ten years or so, I have been largely unmoved and insensitive to the need expressed by a growing number of women to "get out of the house," "find themselves," or "go to law school," but that lack of sensitivity on my part is now a thing of the past.

My transformation came in a blinding flash of light while I was standing up the other evening at our kitchen counter making some potato chips disappear. (It is a well-known scientific fact that food eaten in a standing position metabolizes almost twice as fast as the same-size portions ingested while seated.) So as to avoid responding to shrieks from my wiry wife that I was going to "ruin my supper," I feigned distraction by reading the label on a package of Brown 'n' Serve French Rolls.

I had gone into the text on the package only a short distance before my gorge began to rise in indignation as I realized in what low esteem housewives were held by the supercilious purveyors of these rolls.

The package indicated straightaway that the bakers of these particular rolls considered housewives to be cretinous creatures who must be led by the hand through the simplest of tasks. Under the caption "Serving Suggestions" there appeared the following:

> (1) "Remove from bag before heating." Surely, I thought, there are no housewives bright enough to read who would insert the rolls and the bag in an oven. Instruction (2) adjured the confused cooks to "preheat oven to 425°." Suggestion (3) was to "place rolls on ungreased baking sheet." At this point I wondered if a parenthetical warning should be added alerting the housewife not to confuse a baking sheet with a bed sheet. Suggestion (4) was "brush tops with melted butter" and, this time, a parenthetical "before or after baking" was thoughtfully added. It occurred to me that even if they had left off Suggestion (1) about removing the rolls from the bag before heating, the average housewife would figure this out by the time she got to brushing the tops with melted butter. On the other hand, I guess these bakers didn't want to take anything for granted. Suggestion (5) said to bake 7 to 10 minutes, serve and enjoy. This seemed like good advice to me and couldn't, by any reasonable person, be thought to be patronizing. However, just after this instruction there appeared in bold letters yet another warning—"DO NOT PUT THIS BAG IN OVEN."

Perhaps those of you who have not achieved my level of sensitivity will suggest that the instructions were gender neutral, as men in this enlightened age can often be found browning and serving with the best of them, particularly those supersensitive, simpering wimps on *Thirtysomething* who, every time their wife sighs or focuses on infinity, will furrow a husbandly brow and, in a voice oozing with concern, say, "Honey, are you OK?"

Well, it may be true that the drafters of the serving suggestions didn't have the softer sex in mind in promulgating their overweening advisories, but I can't imagine a manufacturer beginning instructions on how to start a lawn mower, for example, by specifying, "First, take lawn mower out of crate."

As a newly awakened "sensitive person," I for one bitterly resent the vision of womanhood suggested by the sellers of these brown 'n' serve rolls—i.e., a sleepy, slack-jawed, glassy-eyed *hausfrau* who, still in her chenille bathrobe at suppertime, stumbles into the kitchen after an arduous day of watching soap operas and game shows, needing to be taken by the hand and instructed as to how to perform the simplest of tasks.

Women of the world unite! You have nothing to lose but your "serving suggestions." There is no good reason why you should suffer such scorn, ridicule, and public abuse. After all, you're not the vice president of the United States.

"Enough," as Elizabeth Taylor said in declining a recent marriage proposal, "is enough."

August 4, 1989

TV or Not TV

Well, the results of the polling are in and the results are, in a word, shocking.

A recent study by the National Endowment for the Arts revealed that people are reading less, and that those who are still reading are reading thrillers, romances, and science fiction rather than works by "serious" writers. The study also revealed that readership among young adults—those supersensitive thirtysomethings—has dropped severely in the past two decades and that adults spend four times more leisure time with the TV or radio than with reading materials.

My own private studies have revealed that the average lineman on a college football team has difficulty reading his own name on his locker and even the running backs (whose SAT scores, unlike those of the linemen, are often well above room temperature) either (1) move their lips when they read, (2) furrow their brows and use their fingers, or (3) combine all of the foregoing.

SARTUS RESARTUS
The Brothers Karamazoy
BEOWULF AND THE SASS MENAGERIE
BLATZ
JACK DAVIS

Noted academicians from Yale to the Austell Institute of Chiropractic and Auto Upholstery are wringing their hands, tearing their hair, and renting their garments over this sorry development. (Another recent study on renting garments revealed that on some college campuses an English professor could rent a tweed sport coat for as much as three dollars a day provided it smelled of pipe smoke and had leather elbow patches.)

While these academic Chicken Littles beat their breasts and cry aloud as to what may be causing this calamitous decline in readership of serious literature, I, with the curious and sometimes blinding insight which is second nature to persons with a superabundance of common, or as it is sometimes called in west Georgia, "walking around," sense can pinpoint the reason for it with absolute certainty.

I predicted many years ago that we would soon find ourselves in this sorry state of affairs because of the invention and widespread distribution of the remote-control television device or, as my wife refers to it, "that damned flipper."

What chance do classics like *Crime and Punishment*, *Remembrance of Things Past*, *Ulysses* and *The Sass Menagerie* (Longstreet Press, $14.95 in hardback and available at fine bookstores everywhere) have against a sixty-channel cable TV hookup and a remote-control device that permits today's type-A viewers to do a fly pattern through all channels in under forty-five seconds? To ask the question is to answer it.

Even widely known intellectuals like myself have been increasingly inclined to eschew worthwhile reading for the ability to watch four movies, the Playboy Channel, and televised meetings of the Atlanta Library Board simultaneously with only the flick of a thumb. There is, one must concede, an occasional personality so thoroughly torpid that it can withstand the temptation of the almost limitless pleasures offered by remote-control television. If my wife, for example, by random chance or threat of divorce, should gain control of "the damned flipper," she will sit before the television in a state of narcoleptic rapture and watch the same channel for three or four minutes at a stretch. The woman has absolutely no intellectual curiosity. But for most of us the call of the cable is so strong as to preempt other forms of more taxing mental endeavor.

I think it goes without saying, however, that even those of us who are beguiled by the wonders and possibilities for intellectual stimulation offered by remote-control devices would profit in the long run through a return to worthwhile reading. Taking this fact as a given, what then must be done to staunch the gushing of literary lifeblood now taking place through the precipitous decline in serious readers?

The answer is obvious. As in the case with every flaw in the social system, the situation must be addressed and corrected by legislation. Congress should promptly hold hearings on TV flippers and should either (1) ban them outright, (2) require the users to pay a stiff license fee, or (3) give income tax credits for reading worthwhile literature such as *Moby Dick*, *The Iliad*, *Plutarch's Lives*, *The Sass Menagerie* (Longstreet Press, $14.95 in hardback and available at fine bookstores everywhere), etc.

Every day the government delays taking decisive legislative action increases the certainty that successive generations of Americans will have the attention span of a water bug and will have body contours approximating a Lazy Boy recliner chair. The ennobling benefits of reading serious literature will be totally eroded.

I fear, too, that if some severe measures are not taken soon, grown people will begin to carry remote control devices in their pockets throughout the day and stroke them for peace of mind, much in the manner that some first graders continue to take corners of their baby blankets to school or Captain Queeg fondled his steel marbles during moments of stress.

Those gentle readers who haven't abandoned this essay in favor of *World Wrestling Federation*, *Dr. Ruth*, or *Family Feud* by this point, are doubtless asking, "What can I, an average concerned citizen, do about this growing problem?" Well, for one thing, you can get your butt out of the Lazy Boy recliner and rush out to invest heavily in some worthwhile literature, such as *The Brothers Karamazov, Sartor Resartus, Beowulf,* or *The Sass Menagerie* (Longstreet Press, $14.95 in hardback and available at fine bookstores everywhere).

And from this day forth you can let the rallying cry go forward into the halls, corridors, and cloakrooms of Congress and throughout the nation, "We need a whole lot more of Dostoevski and a lot less Danielle Steel!"

November 3, 1989

Just an Old Stone Who's Rolled over the Hill

There are some people in this world, my wife specifically springs to mind, who would pay to see a root canal if getting a ticket to the event were a virtual impossibility. It was on the crest of just such an implausible wave that she and I and a group of friends and revelers found ourselves at the recent Rolling Stones concert. Doggedly taking leave of our senses, we elbowed our way through a teeming throng of teeny boppers, T-shirt hucksters, ticket scalpers, and other middle-aged crazies to take in the Atlanta stop on the Steel Wheels Tour.

Having just survived my fifty-third birthday the day before, I was glumly trying to persuade my wizened bride that I was not shaped for such sportive tricks when she, overcome by a spasm of enthusiasm, insisted I hoist her up on my shoulders "to get in the spirit of things." Only by pointing out that we were still in the parking lot of the Varsity and reminding her that I had left my truss in the glove compartment of the car, was I able to keep her from actually climbing up on my withers.

The concert was held in the open at Georgia Tech's Grant Field and, I have to confess, I can't remember seeing such excitement and electricity on those grounds since Coach Bobby Dodd would, on occasion, wait until fourth down to punt the football.

As indicated earlier, our group was a bit long in the tooth and, as we squeezed into our seats, some callow youth behind us muttered, "There must have been a breakout at Wesley Woods."

However, if the Clearasil crowd found pleasure in mocking their elders, they needed to look no further than the stage where the aging Stones were plying their cacophonous trade. The drummer, who I'm told is not the oldest of the geriatric jumping jacks, looked like George Burns, while another in this motley crew (I think his name was Keith Motley) was the living embodiment of "rode hard and put up wet."

According to my daughter, Nona Begonia, who was serving as an interpreter to our group, a third Stone, Bill Wyman, is precisely my age though he had recently taken a 19-year-old as his bride. As an aside which would be of great interest to those who inhabit the mountain wilds of north Georgia, Wyman's son was dating the 19-year-old's mother. If they marry, his mother-in-law could become his daughter-in-law which, though confusing in the extreme, would certainly cut down on the number of Christmas gifts under the tree.

The main Stone, of course, is the cadaverous, rubber-lipped Mick Jagger, who may be living proof that Barney Fife and Martha Raye were more than "just friends." The man looks old, the man is old. Beyond that, he needs to call up Michael Jackson and find out who does his lips.

The star of the show as far as I was concerned was the massive set which appeared to be a replica of the Pompidou Museum in Paris and which upstaged the Stones by alternately belching smoke and blinking fire. In the middle of one number,

"Honky Tonk Woman," two pneumatic Macy's Parade-type inflatable strumpets were blown up to gigantic proportions. I thought these towering tarts stole the show.

Meanwhile, all around us frantic teenagers, thirtysomethings, and a very generous segment of borderline AARP prospects jerked convulsively to the screeching of the Steel Wheels as the Stones ground through their musical gears and a brown cloud of smoke smelling suspiciously like someone smoking a tennis shoe billowed softly over the stadium.

After two and a half hours of sustained caterwauling, I recognized only two numbers—the aforementioned "Honky Tonk Woman" and "Satisfaction" (as in "I can't *get* no ..."). The other songs (it may have been the same song repeated over and over) went on interminably and, three-quarters of the way through each of them, I began to have anxiety attacks fearing that the Senile Stones had forgotten the ending and that we would be trapped in Grant Field until the towering speakers self-destructed.

The convulsive motions of the crowd confirmed another long-held suspicion of mine which is that most Wasp music lovers, whatever their ages, are basically arrhythmic. As Richard Pryor once asked cogently, "What are those white people dancing to...the words?"

From the moment the first mind-shattering note was struck to the very end of the concert, logic and comfort were totally abandoned as no concertgoer remained in his (or as the newly sensitive would say, "his-or-her") seat. Throughout the whole blooming musical miasma, everyone in the stadium stood on their feet except for those in the infield who stood on their folding chairs.

Finally, and mercifully, midway through what we thought to be the last number, the husband of one of the oldsters in our group leaned over to shout that he thought his wife was "bladder dead" and asked my assistance in getting her to the ladies room at a nearby Gulf station. The poor woman, thwarted by a combination of old age and modesty, had previously refused to crash the men's rooms of the stadium in the customary fashion of young concert-going debutantes of the day, and had gone into something of a terminal squirm midway through the concert. At least we know why *she* was moving to a different beat.

As we helped the tight-lipped, urgent-eyed victim up the packed aisles, I vowed to myself that I wouldn't attend another concert unless Fred Waring and the Pennsylvanians announced their 1990 Prune Tour and decided that I was, to borrow a line from a current Randy Travis tune, "just an old stone who's rolled over the hill."

The bottom line for Steel Wheels is that while a Rolling Stone may gather no moss, nobody said anything about liver spots.

December 2, 1989

How's Your Hammacher Schlemmer Hanging?

I wish the activist legions would give a rest to reproduction, fur-wearing, and the greenhouse effect and turn their guns on mail-order catalogs before it's too late.

In olden days when people did something which identified them as an easy mark capable of being thoroughly mulcted, travelling gypsies would place some sort of secret mark over the door of the unsuspecting pigeon and thereafter hordes of their colleagues would flock by to take advantage of the dupe thus designated.

Nowadays, the same result is achieved when you buy something from a mail-order catalog. Once this happens, the catalog company sends your name and address to a huge underground silo in Junk Mail, Idaho, where it is placed on a Master List. Thereafter your mailman risks a double hernia daily delivering towering stacks of ever-proliferating mail-order catalogs, most of them trumpeting an incredible array of worthless goods.

In last week's barrage, I was struck by a catalog which proved beyond any doubt the low opinion mail-order companies have of their unseen customers. It was from an outfit called Hammacher Schlemmer and offered an astounding assortment of useless items for shoppers who are too lazy to forge through the teeming malls themselves or who are candidates for the South Georgia Home for the Profligate Rich.

Although I didn't know what "Hammacher Schlemmer" meant, I had been introduced to the company about twenty-five years ago while in New York City on legal business with a former acquaintance, Richard A. Allison (not his real name), who was known to be a card-carrying member of the idle rich.

Allison, though a native of the Hookworm and Pellagra Belt in Southwest Alabama, was born with a silver spoon in his mouth. (Aside from a slight speech impediment and excessive drooling when agitated, the plucky Allison has managed to overcome this handicap.) He was always quick to point out that he had attended Princeton, and while I don't have anything against Ivy Leaguers, they do have an unfortunate tendency to speak as though they are dictating to a stonecutter and will often say things like, "be that as it may."

As we roamed the city, Allison insisted we go by Hammacher Schlemmer so that he could get some "great and unusual gift" for his father. I can't remember what he bought him (the options I still recall were tungsten socks, vibrating underwear, a foot-operated fish scaler, and a hand-carried portable toilet), but I do remember being left with the overall impression that this establishment was clearly a place for people with more money than critical judgment.

In reviewing their current catalog, I discovered that in the intervening twenty-five years, nothing much had changed at Hammacher Schlemmer.

For the affluent mafioso, the catalog offers a remote-control car starter which also "activates your car's headlights and sounds a locating whistle allowing you to find your car in a crowded parking lot." Other "must have" items included a "snore-reducing pillow" which, from the look of it, would be most effective when held tightly over the snorer's face for five or ten minutes, an orthopedic pet bed (for those who may be reluctant to take their animals to a chiropractor), a battery-operated nose-and-ear hair trimmer (guaranteed to cause even the most jaded dinner companion to sit up and take notice), moisture-absorbing chamois socks, a hands-free snowball maker and a solar-ventilated golf cap with a built-in fan for the forehead (for those seeking to establish themselves as the ultimate dork).

In the section modestly titled "The Future Now," Hammacher Schlemmer features a vacuum-powered insect disposal system which "lets you quickly capture and dispose of insects at a comfortable distance without requiring direct contact or leaving any mess." This causes me to believe that the old-fashioned fly swatter will soon go the way of the buggy whip for all who can afford the modestly priced ($49.95 with six disposable cartridges at an additional $29.95) vacuum. Finally, they offer an ultrasonic dog repeller which "produces a high-frequency sound wave which will deter bothersome or attacking dogs." If their research department can ever perfect this item so it can be used against insurance agents and telephone solicitors, I think they may be on to something.

Provided an exception can be carved out for the tastefully designed and beautifully presented catalog titled "Victoria's Secret," I would favor immediate legislation requiring criminal sanctions for the distribution or possession of mail-order catalogs.

And, for those of you who are getting up to call or write your legislator, you can tell him or her I have made diligent inquiry and have learned that Hammacher Schlemmer is German for "There's one born every minute."

February 9, 1990

Broccoli? Just Say No

Many political commentators (particularly that bunch of geezers who sit around in a semicircle on public television and all talk and shout at the same time) are questioning whether the presidency of the United States, having been weakened for eight consecutive years by an administration that was either napping or suffering memory lapses, could ever be restored in the public eye to its former position of strength and high resolve.

I think President Bush, with his lightning-quick and resolute preemptive strike on broccoli, put that question to rest once and for all as far as his administration is concerned. Sensing correctly that Middle America was growing weary of our country's lack of a firm policy on obscure and bad-tasting vegetables, the president took firm and decisive action, having said privately to a few key cabinet members, "It's time we stopped pussyfooting around on the broccoli question." His move was thought by some to be even more courageous than that of the previous

JACK DAVIS

administration's invasion of Granada. "After all," said Defense Secretary Dick Cheney on a special edition of *Nightline* ("Veggies: The Evil Empire?"), "there are a helluva lot more broccoli growers than there were enemy forces in Granada."

Cheney, in an account given to a few Washington insiders, told of a tense all-night gathering in the Oval Office when the president, after having heard arguments from all of his senior advisers, set his jaw, put down a pork rind on which he had been gnawing, and said, "Guys, I think it's time we kicked a little asparagus here."

Military analysts, ringing their hands like Chicken Little, wondered aloud and in print if a domino effect might result with other vegetables such as artichokes, cauliflower, and arugula being targeted for future action by the tough-talking Bush administration. President Gorbachev, distracted by matters of lesser moment, such as demands for independence by the churls in Lithuania (the churls, though an ethnic minority in Lithuania, control most of the important posts in government because of their uncanny but inexplicable ability to score high on civil service exams), was taken completely off guard by Bush's bold maneuver. Sensing that Bush had stolen a march in this critical area of global consequence, Gorbochev rushed on television and said lamely that he never really cared for beets or red cabbage, but it was too little, too late.

The powerful broccoli interests, caught flat-footed by the president's surprise thrust, finally attempted to retaliate by sending ten tons of broccoli (with an estimated street value of $82.14) to Washington, but the shipment was intercepted by the District of Columbia police, leading to later charges by the *National Enquirer* that Mayor Marion Barry had been observed in an Alamo Plaza Motel in north Virginia smoking some of the confiscated stalks.

Predictably, the president's stand was characterized by the Arabs as pro-Israel, causing Israel to make demands on the U.S. for more economic and military aid. Meanwhile, the PLO used the increased media coverage to deny persistent rumors that Yassir Arafat and Ringo Starr are really the same person.

The nation's press, in a typical spasm of establishment bashing, trumpeted that the president's move would cause great harm to minorities and the homeless but admitted that it might be some months before they could really figure out just why this was so.

Speaking only for the little man (an increasingly difficult task given the fact that my wattles have almost completely obscured the knot on my necktie), I can only say that for someone who for fifty-three years has eaten only three green foods (jelly beans, lime Life Savers and, in 1956, a suspicious-looking cold cut that had been languishing way past its expiration date in the fraternity house refrigerator), what President Bush has done makes me proud to be a carbohydrate-stuffing, snack-fooding, red-meat-eating American. Praise the Lord and pass the mashed potatoes and we'll all be free!

March 31, 1990

Time Is Money

Call me the Apostle of the Obvious, but I find the *Wall Street Journal* a bit gray and drab (not to be confused with a large Atlanta law firm by the same name). I suspect my impression results in large part by reason of the fact that most of my savings are tied up in a war bond my grandparents gave me in 1943, while the rest are in a bank Christmas club account which pays no interest.

Beyond that, the *WSJ* has no sports section, no funny papers, and no TV listings. However, on a rare and random occasion, it can cough up an interesting kernel or two for the alert reader.

Just last week, as I browsed through an abandoned issue in an airport waiting room, I came across an extraordinary advertisement offering "pre-owned watches, including Rolex, Cartier, Patek-Phillipe [which, until then, I had thought was a French milk of magnesia], etc. at prices starting as low as $400."

The ad featured a beefy-looking pilot in front of a propeller-driven airplane who was described as a "captain with a major American airline." The ad went on to say that Captain Strow (obviously not his real name) "could easily afford a new watch, but he, as thousands before him, opted for the wiser choice...PRE-OWNED!" The ad was placed by Grafstein & Co. ("wholesalers to the Trade since 1939"), with establishments in Santa Ana, Beverly Hills, and New York.

To illustrate just what bargains were available to wristwatch *arrivistes*, the ad featured a photo of a Rolex SS Gold Datejust which retailed originally for $3,650 but which could be snapped up from Grafstein for a mere $1,790. The ad didn't say what the "SS" stood for, but one assumes "Silly Sap," i.e., one who would pay $3,650 in the first place for a wristwatch which had gold pimples instead of numbers.

It is absolutely mind-boggling (though some have observed that my mind boggles more easily than most) to imagine a business enterprise dealing in used watches which could afford to advertise in the *Wall Street Journal*.

Come with us now through the magic of a sick imagination to the plush Beverly Hills showroom of Grafstein & Co. as some *parvenu* seeks to certify his sociability by upgrading his timepiece.

A sales person dressed in a pair of pinstripe pants and a black swallow-tailed coat is cooing to the customer, "This particular Rolex was previously owned by a basketball player who turned professional after only three years of college and thus never learned to tell time. I mean the watch has barely been looked at. It can be yours for a mere $1,790."

> Customer (good naturedly): "What's the 'SS' for? Silly Sap?" Salesperson (haughtily): "Don't be *jejune*. Besides, that gag was used earlier in the column."

The clear danger (other than a third reference to "SS") is that this trafficking in expensive used watches represents a very dangerous trend. As anyone who has given the matter any serious thought can appreciate, obscenely priced watches have a very important place in our modern society.

Without them some chump sitting next to an important person would not know that he was a chump and the person next to him was an important person unless the important person was able to flaunt a wristwatch costing roughly as much as a new four-door Hyundai. What, then, will become of the social order if every upstart can appear to be an important person by simply buying a Rolex oyster *secondhand*?

It's critically important that important people have a clear-cut method of declaring their importance and, while alligator attaché cases, Gucci anythings, and car phones help, nothing else makes such a supercilious statement so succinctly as a stratospherically priced timepiece. (You may wonder at the excessive alliteration in this paragraph. It is intentional. Recent studies by Masters and Johnson have revealed that a significant number of female newspaper readers actually become aroused by a succession of sibilant sounds.)

I don't have any answer for all this, but it's certainly something for you to think about when you're not heavily engaged in other high-minded and challenging activities, like watching the *Newlywed Game* or looking through the *Wall Street Journal* for something interesting to read.

May 21, 1990

Ah, Sweet Mysteries of Golf

Oscar Wilde once described the sport of fox hunting as "the unspeakable in full pursuit of the inedible." Modernizing and paraphrasing, one might describe golf as "the uncoordinated in dogged pursuit of the unachievable."

There are, to be sure, a small knot of golf's practitioners who do achieve a slippery and temporal grip on the slithery sport and sometimes shoot par. Those people are referred to by wannabe golfer Lewis Grizzard as knowing "the secret." Grizzard, upon seeing a par golfer in action, will mutter knowingly and bitterly, "He's one of 'em. He knows the secret," certain but unhappy in the knowledge that the par golfer would rather have his appendix removed with a rusty niblick than share the secret with the rest of us.

Only a race of people as dour and ascetic as the Scots could have conceived an enterprise as masochistic as golf. The term itself derives from the Caledonian word *golffe,* meaning incredible pain, public humiliation, or self-flagellation.

Next to making a serious speech to a D.A.R. Convention with your fly open, golf is the most humbling and embarrassing endeavor known to our society.

Why reasonably intelligent adults submit themselves so unrelentingly to its rigors ranks with other mysteries of cosmic consequence, such as: (1) Is TV wrestling fake? (2) Why does the other line always move faster? and (3) What is the average IQ of those people who put little stuffed animals with suction cups for paws on their car windows?

Not only is the sport itself a multinational obsession, recent forecasts by the internationally renowned Cobb County School of Economics, Electrolysis, and Bikini Waxing predict that by the year 2000 over one-half of our GNP will be spent on golf equipment and related accoutrements such as head covers for putters, Day-Glo-colored knickers, golf balls of incredibly bilious hues, golf bags sufficient in size to house a family of boat people, and high-tech golf clubs with shafts made from everything from beryllium (a new miracle alloy made of barium enemas, aluminum, and ground-up Toyota parts) to radioactive waste.

The incredible eagerness of rabid golfers to spend money on the craze knows no bounds. Early reports indicate that a newly released book on golf, *Does a Wild Bear Chip in the Woods?* by the previously mentioned "Muse of Moreland," Lewis Grizzard, himself a 12-handicapper, is selling like hotcakes (this in spite of the fact that one reviewer claimed the syrup and butter made it a "messy read").

If I may be permitted a personal aside, I would mention that Grizzard (ever alert for extended filler) included in the book an unexpurgated reprint of an article on golf from *Augusta Magazine* written by my brother, Michael Parker Steed (actually the article was printed in block letters with crayon, but I'm coming to that).

"Mike," as we all call him, deserves all the encouragement we can give him. Just two years ago we learned he was addicted to those letters in *Penthouse* and we had to send him to Tifton to the Georgia Baptist Home for the Easily Aroused. At one point he had read so many of those letters he couldn't even lick a stamp without getting keyed up.

He's back on the streets now, a bit tense but otherwise fully recovered, and the magazine article reprinted in Grizzard's book was thought to be a major breakthrough in his treatment. Buy the book. It will help your insight into the mysteries of golf and, more important, it will help us keep Mike at home where he belongs.

June 6, 1990

Closing the Bluster Gap

I hate to sound a note of caution when our president has struck such a marvelously resounding chord in the jingoistic loins of our angry and aroused nation, but, being fully aware that the opening battles of our Arabian adventure are going to be fought on *Nightline* and refereed by Ted Koppel, I have a genuine concern that is beginning to scab and fester (not to be confused with a group of Cobb County urologists by the same name).

I don't suggest for a minute that our troops can't overcome the Iraqi forces facing them. I am fully convinced that the 101st Airborne Division could, if unleashed and unfettered, kick Saddam Hussein's butt so badly he would spend the rest of his life walking around on his elbows.

No, it's in the area of florid rhetoric that I believe the United States is experiencing a *bluster* gap.

In terms of threats, taunts and gibes, the Iraqis are way ahead on points. At the drop of a fez, Saddam Hussein and his

HOGAN
JACK DAVIS

minions will spout rhetorical flourishes that absolutely take one's breath away in terms of their hyperbolic and vehement audacity.

Before our troops could disembark (military for "get off the boat") in Saudi Arabia, Saddam and his coterie launched into flowery fulminations promising to "pluck out their eyes" or "spill rivers of blood that not even the sands of the great desert can absorb." Watching his nightly monologue, one imagines a staff of sweaty writers sitting in the back of the tent coming up with curses like "May a dyspeptic camel defile your tupperware" or "May Roseanne Barr sit on your Pop-Tarts."

Our leader, on the other hand, will preface his responses with "Golly" or "Gee," and then go on to give some nasal whitebread response that wouldn't intimidate a determined Avon lady. White House insiders confide that in private his responses are significantly more salty, ranging from "Oh, yeah?" to "Who says so?" or, when he is particularly incensed, "Your Mother!"

It seems to me we are in serious danger of losing the battle of bluster, and my advice is to immediately create a new cabinet level position called the Secretary of Imprecations whose sole duty would be to appear on the Seven O'Clock News and answer Hussein's rantings measure for measure.

We need look no further than the ranks of our ever-choleric television wrestlers to find our man. All the president has to do is flip to Channel 47 and *World Wrestling Federation* to find someone who can give Hussein the old what for.

My personal choice for the position would be Hulk Hogan. Hogan, a maniacal-looking taxpayer with a perpetual tan and greasy dancing pectorals, is currently in an ongoing shouting match with a bearded behemoth called simply "Earthquake" (though that could be a nickname) as they bait each other over the upcoming and eagerly awaited "Summer Slam." It is a wondrous and sometimes frightening moment when the fulminating mastodons stand nose to nose and shout threats filled with passion, imagination, and a fair amount of spittle at each other, while the announcer tries his best to look serious and ponder the cosmic implications of who will take the zircon-encrusted heavyweight belt from whom.

While President Bush and the 101st Airborne Division will certainly do the job if and when the Summer Slam in Saudi starts in earnest, I think that in the meantime we all can agree that it's better to be shouting than shooting and that we need to have Hulk Hogan up front if we really expect anyone to read our lips.

August 24, 1990

In Search of Fiscal Rectitude

With all the fanfare of a World Wrestling Federation match between Andre the Giant and King Kong Bundy, the president and Congress have taken on the budget in what appears to be a best two-out-of-three-falls match. Their first effort at Andrews Air Force Base was abortive to say the least. (Speaking of abortion, I am reliably informed by persons close to newly confirmed Supreme Court justice David Souter that he privately opposes abortions except in the case of rape, incest, or marriage between Roseanne Barr and Andrew Dice Clay.)

The president and Congress, in round two of this mad grapple in search of fiscal rectitude, have simply declared the result in advance and then set about to flail around till they achieve it.

It occurred to this writer that asking Congress for advice on how to cut spending is like asking Maynard Jackson for tips on bungee jumping. With that assumption firmly in mind, it seems reasonable to suggest that perhaps an outsider's perspective might be useful to our nation's leaders as they stage this fiscal Armageddon.

The basic problem is, of course, that Congress simply will not make any spending cuts. They have for decades adopted the philosophy so long and urgently espoused by my sinewy spouse: "If you want it, you need it."

Thus, cooler and more deliberative heads will have to come up with revenue measures which do not involve actual spending cuts. To demonstrate the power of a non-Potomac perspective, I herewith offer just a few:

(1) Bake sales. With the increasing number of women in Congress, this is a real revenue-raising possibility. I don't mean to sound sexist by associating women with cooking (I personally tend to associate them with expensive restaurants), but I certainly wouldn't want to eat anything that Ted Kennedy had touched.

(2) Turn out the lights when leaving a room or, for that matter, a military installation. With our entire armed forces in sunny Saudi, there is no reason to leave the lights on at military bases all over the U.S. In point of fact, there's no reason to leave the lights on in the Capitol either, as Congress has been in the dark for years.

(3) Voluntary contributions by citizens. I'm suggesting that all citizens turn in their accumulated pennies to balance the budget. A recent study by the Cobb County Center for Strategic Thought and Take-Out Chicken suggests that in every household in the United States there is a huge container of pennies and that if all of these could be sent to Washington at the same time, the deficit would be cut by as much as fifty billion dollars. Moreover, the center estimates it would take the members of Congress over five years to wrap the pennies, thus preventing them from passing any new spending legislation in the meantime.

(4) Clipping coupons. I don't know how much the government has been paying for apple and cinnamon flavored Jetsons

Cereal but, if recent scandals in Defense Department spending tell us anything, I'll bet it's plenty. By merely sifting through the towering stack of valuable coupon offers which accompany each Sunday newspaper, the government could save seventy-five cents on each box of Jetsons, thirty cents on any one six-pack of Jell-O Pudding Snacks, and thirty-five cents on five cans of Fresh Catch ("dolphin-safe seafood for cats available in seven delicious varieties").

(5) A national lottery. Ed McMahon should be immediately named Secretary of Avarice (Department of Fat Chance) to head a national lottery. There is no reason why the states should be the only ones to prosper from government-sanctioned exploitation of greed.

(6) Celebrity Auctions. These affairs have proved both effective and enjoyable for charitable fund-raisers, and I'm sure there are plenty of people who would pay big money to go to a MENSA meeting with Dan Quayle or a Robert Maplethorpe exhibit with Jesse Helms.

These and many other trenchant suggestions toward national fiscal responsibility and tax equity can be found in the pages of my soon-to-be-published book, *Up Your Bracket* (Simon & Lipshutz, $21.95 hardback. Also available in cassettes).

October 18, 1990

Politicians Should Be Flushed with Success

With the cost of running election campaigns for state offices now approaching the size of the defense budget or Bill Cosby's take-home pay, it occurred to me during the most recent political hysteria that it is high time to take some drastic measures to reduce the pocketbook pain endured by the candidates and those hapless souls who are called on to fund their interminable and tedious quests for votes.

Voters, quite naturally, become a bit suspicious when candidates who are contending for jobs that pay less than the annual salary of the average Herbal-Life distributor spend multimillions in campaign advertising, all of which look pretty much alike. In almost every TV ad the shirt-sleeved candidates appear, oozing sincerity and surrounded by swarms of smiling children, old folks, and minorities. It's mostly the same old crowd telling us how they're going to deliver us from the same old crowd.

Beyond that, scientific research has revealed that prospective

DON'T BLAME ME
I VOTED FOR BUSH
JACK DAVIS

voters, after having been bombarded by TV campaign advertisements over a long period of time, become convinced that the candidates are starting to look alike, a dynamic which is somewhat similar to the phenomenon of old married people who begin to resemble each other.

Not only is all of this horribly expensive, but the plethora of TV political ads take up valuable space that otherwise would be available for more important commercial messages such as, to give just one example, the one with Fran Tarkenton and some square-jawed young motivational guru who looks like Arnold Schwarzenegger before steroids. Because of all of the political ads cluttering the airwaves, programmers are forced to air this paradigm of advertising sincerity in the predawn hours in the upper reaches of cable television, where the old quarterback can be found earnestly asking the motivational guru just how he came to possess the sum of all human knowledge, learned to cope with all of life's problems, became a success at everything he undertook while, at the same time, managing to rid himself of unwanted nostril hair. The answers, we are assured, are revealed in audiotapes, videocassettes, and associated pamphlets which may be had by members of the general public if they will only cough up $179.95 plus tax and handling.

Vitally important commercial messages like these probably could be aired during prime time if it weren't for the relentless succession of political commercials preempting all the good spots.

In the interest of improving the electoral process, freeing the airwaves of boring political ads, shortening the political campaigns and saving the candidates and their public-spirited backers literally millions of dollars, I am prepared to advance a modest proposal which involves a new method of political campaigning and voting. Yes, you heard it here first, the Steed Hydraulic Electoral System.

My system would involve legislation which would prohibit all candidates from soliciting or spending any money for their campaigns. Instead, opposing candidates would get to appear one time on a statewide television and radio simulcast and in thirty minutes explain why the voters should choose them for high public office. At the end of the thirty-minute session, a special signal would be given and, at that moment, all voters who favored that particular candidate would race to their bathrooms and flush their toilets. The same procedure would be employed for the next candidate at the end of his harangue.

Water and sewerage systems from Rabun Gap to Tybee Light would then dutifully record the respective pressure drops and report the winners by telephone to the secretary of state who could announce the results in minutes. This would also spare us the tedium involved in all those election-night TV specials where the regular anchorpersons keep asking Claibourne Darden, "Claibourne, what does all this mean?"

In fact, unless someone was in a great hurry to find out who won, we could even bypass the secretary of state's declaration and just announce the winners by printing their names on the next month's water bill.

Backwoods voters and those in areas of Cobb County without indoor plumbing would, of course, vote by absentee ballot but, since the Steed Hydraulic Electoral System of voting has a margin of error of from 10 to 15 percent, those votes would not be counted, as it is unlikely that they would affect the result in any case.

The millions of dollars thus saved could be used to buy state lottery tickets or motivational tapes, with the result that the public schools, old quarterbacks, and motivational gurus would be greatly enriched.

The system is simple, efficient, and reliable and, in my judgment, would have a cathartic effect on voter apathy. Beyond that, it would give new meaning to the term "flushed with success."

November 15, 1990

War Is Hell; Media Are Worse

Like every other red-blooded American (or, in the case of some scattered demonstrators who are obviously throwbacks to an earlier war, pink-blooded Americans), I have been spending an inordinate amount of time bumping around the TV channels eager for news of the war.

The only firm conclusion I have reached in all of this is that the military should stop the daily news briefings until the press can come up with better questions.

The standard inquiries, asked over and over and over, often in a whiny, accusatorial tone, can be summed up as follows:

(1) "Haven't you folks really been lying through your teeth when you told us the war would be over in a few days?" This causes what is now almost a canned response by Defense Secretary Cheney, General Schwarzkopf, General Johnston, or whoever else is being interrogated, to the effect that, "We have been very careful from the outset to avoid any implication that

the war would be short in duration or over in a hurry." One reporter, driven more by persistence than intelligence, insisted in a tone so snide and nasty that Sam Donaldson would have twitched in envy, "Well, Egypt's President Mubarak said the war would be over in ten days. What about that?" The obviously exasperated spokesman replied, "You'll just have to check with Mr. Mubarak about that."

(2) "When will the ground war begin and just where will we attack?" As incredibly asinine as such a question might seem to anyone with a trace of walking-around sense, it is asked, in one form or another, over and over and over with the relentlessness of a small child on a long trip asking, "Are we there yet, Daddy?"

(3) Over this past weekend, the favorite question was nuclear in nature as in "What if Saddam Hussein uses chemical agents, will we retaliate with nuclear weapons and, if not, why not?" Even though those being interviewed answered with responses which ranged from firmly refusing to consider such a grisly hypothetical to simply rolling their eyeballs heavenward, the fourth estate persisted with the inquiry to great lengths and on all fronts. I'm becoming increasingly afraid that this war, like many political conventions, cannot generate enough action to sate the voracious reporting appetites of the droves of newspaper men and women sent to cover it.

When the media have absolutely no facts at hand or have beaten the available facts to a quivering pulp, they resort to lassoing some psychologist from a nearby college campus and asking for psychological profiles of Saddam Hussein. Over the past few weeks I learned the following from these bush-league headshrinkers:

(1) Saddam Hussein sleeps with a night light. This might indicate an incipient lack of courage and could possibly explain the fact that he has not responded to our attacks.

(2) Saddam Hussein is very bright but doesn't do well on standardized tests. We don't know what this means in terms of future tactics, but it will definitely weigh heavily against his

chances of getting into a good graduate school after the war.

(3) The mustache Saddam wears is fake and he has a habit of regularly misplacing it. This could indicate low self-esteem and a diminished supply of blood to the brain.

(4) Saddam likes to "dress up" wearing a wide array of outfits ranging from traditional Arab robes to camouflaged merry widows and garter belts. This could suggest that the Allied forces might consider a well-timed B-52 run over Frederick's of Baghdad.

(5) Saddam has a lively sense of humor, as evidenced by the fact that he once alleged in a nationwide state of the union address that the Ayatollah Khomeini and Gabby Hayes were the same person. Western observers knew that he was making the remark in jest because it was followed by a rim shot from the drummer in the Palace band. His sense of humor suggests that he may spend a good deal of time watching televised Pentagon news briefings and laughing uproariously at the questions.

Stay tuned.

February 11, 1991

Open Diapers and Other Life-Altering Adventures

While passing through New York's LaGuardia Airport last week I took the opportunity to slip into a bookstore and, looking furtively over both shoulders, picked up a copy of Kitty Kelly's *Unauthorized Biography of Nancy Reagan.*

Fearing that someone I knew might see me carrying that dubious piece of literary business, I repaired straightaway to the men's room, where I opened my suitcase and tucked it down between the dirty dress shirts and hotel towels.

While in the men's room, I came face-to-face with a sign which offered the ultimate proof—if any proof was wanted—that the times, indeed, they are a changin'. It bore the throbbing legend, "This table is provided for changing babies' diapers."

"What in the world have we come to?" I exclaimed, causing a man next to me to give me an anxious look and quickly dart away.

The idea of a diaper-changing table in a men's room might

cause Phil Donahue to swoon in a supersensitive rapture but, as for me, it provoked the strongest sort of feeling that the shadows were getting longer and that I was terribly out of touch.

When my full-time children were still in untrained state, I would go to any lengths to avoid a confrontation with an open diaper, often feigning deafness or insanity and fabricating all sorts of elaborate excuses as to why I couldn't engage in such a grisly enterprise. When left alone by their mother for any extended period, I would wind up in an eye-watering panic, carrying a soggy babe about at arm's length for hours to avoid changing a diaper.

My theory was that until children were potty trained they should be kept in wire bottomed cages. A group of behavioral scientists in Cobb County tried this in the mid-1960's but determined that it led to severe personality changes in the children and that many of them were inclined in their teenage years to axe-murder their sleeping parents or, worse yet, run for public office. My offspring took their revenge on my diaperphobia by creating intercollegiate records in parking tickets and bank overdrafts but happily never resorted to anything lethal or political in nature.

When I told my law partner, Byron "Whiplash" Attridge, how large our sensitivity gap had grown by relating the diaper-changing table sighting in the men's room, he said, "Hell, that's nothing. I've heard that there have been reported cases of some of these yuppie husbands actually going into the delivery room and videotaping live births!"

"My guess," he went on, "is that the doctors are too busy to catch them, but how would you like to go to a dinner party and have one of them tell you, 'Oh, before we eat, let's go into the den and watch Jennifer having little Mark.'"

I was glad I had bought the Kitty Kelly book because it did contain some startling and myth-shattering revelations about the Reagans. I don't want to go into too much detail, but I did learn that (1) a "close friend" of the Reagans told Ms. Kelly that

"If Ronnie has one more face-lift, his navel is going to pop up over his shirt collar," and (2) after becoming president, Ronald Reagan turned his back on Bonzo because of a personality conflict between the hairy actor and Nancy Reagan and refused to return his phone calls or give him banana money when he was down and out.

About a quarter of the way into Ms. Kelly's book it occurred to me that it would not be entirely inaccurate to say it was the literary equivalent of looking into an open diaper.

April 29, 1991

I Brake for Frogs

Since the Atlanta papers first began covering Dixie like the dew several years after the beginning of time, irate politicians, owners of purported major league franchises, and chicken lovers everywhere have been heard to utter the recurring war cry, "Them lying Atlanta Newspapers!" To those muttering malcontents I say, "Lying *Atlanta* newspapers? What about the lying *Wall Street Journal?*"

Actually, I never said that to any of those choleric and foam-flecked souls. Ever eager to avoid any sort of confrontation which might lead to physical pain, my approach is usually to smile and reply, "Well, I wouldn't know. I only read *Grit* and the *Christian Science Monitor*."

However, while I didn't say it, I did *think* it about the *Wall Street Journal* when I read a recent article in its stolid pages on the perilous sex habits of British toads.

The front page story by "Glynn Mapes" (obviously a fake

SCREECH
CHAZ
TOAD
CROSSING
JACK DAVIS

name) bore the dateline of "Henley-on-Thames, England" and contained the wart-raising revelation that every March, "some 20 million tons of toads are run over by cars" while crossing public roadways to nearby breeding ponds.

Actually, in partial defense of the *WSJ*, the 20 million tons of toads figure came from unnamed "toad experts." (Imagine the unmitigated shame endured by a parent who, when asked by well-meaning friends what their son is doing for a living, must look them in the eye and say, "Actually, Heathcliff is a toad expert." Is it any wonder the British are thought to be in such a precipitous general decline?)

According to the *WSJ*, the annual toad squashing is a dreadful carnage which makes a sickening and dangerous mess of the highways. However, one man's carnage is another man's cause and the account goes on to report that in the United Kingdom alone, some four thousand volunteers of the International Toads on the Roads Society muck about the roadways in rubber boots using plastic pails to carry the endangered toads to safety. My guess is that these people are on the waiting lists as potential protesters for the baby seal, the presidential parkway, and the anti-veal-cutlet protest movements which are currently so overburdened with eager volunteers that they have had to temporarily close their membership ranks.

Enterprising Toads on the Roaders have also constructed six toad tunnels under selected highways to reduce the slithery slaughter.

But back to the question of honesty in journalism and the reporting of the slippery statistic that 20 million tons of toads are run over by cars during the mating season every March.

My bean-counting banker friend, Linden "Double Entry" Longino, took the *WSJ* to task by pointing out in an unacknowledged and unpublished letter to their editors that 20 million tons of toads is, to quote his own mild understatement, "a lot of toads." It is, by his calculation, 40 billion pounds, to be precise and, estimating 20 toads to the pound, he reckons that

800 billion toads are crushed annually in England during the mating season. And, as he cogently points out, these are just the ones that fatefully find themselves "between the treads on the ribiting road to love." Assuming, Longino, continues with the pencil-pushing persistence of a skeptical and gimlet-eyed banker, that only 20 percent of the horny toads are crushed in their passage over the roads (800 billion toads), the annual population would equal 4 trillion toads. With this frightful horror afoot, my guess is that Margaret Thatcher didn't just resign, she fled the country while there was still time.

The relentless Longino, by now drenched in sweat but still hunched over his Hewlett-Packard, summed up his incredulity with this felicitous observation: "It is intuitively obvious to even the most casual observer of nature that the experts you quoted must be Bull frogs. If 4 trillion two-inch-long toads formed an off-road chorus line, this happy host of hopeful horny hoppers would wrap around the world five thousand times—croaking for safe sex."

Like I said, that lying *Wall Street Journal*—sex, lies, and the toadally absurd!

June 26, 1991

Switzerland Uber Alles

I don't want readers to think that I'm off on some sort of vendetta ("vendetta"—*n.* 1. vengeful quarrel; 2. Italian economy car introduced unsuccessfully after World War II) against the *Wall Street Journal.* After all, it's easy to pick on a newspaper with no sports page, comics, or Ann Landers and whose idea of a dynamite above-the-fold headline is "Hennessy Is Retiring at Allied Signal Sooner Than Expected." Even though my recent column debunking claims by the *WSJ* to the effect that eighty billion toads are squashed annually as they cross British roadways to nearby breeding ponds is being quietly promoted for a Pulitzer, I have no ambitions to undertake some sort of jihad against the trusty old business chronicle.

However, I would be derelict if I didn't point out that an increasing number of bubbles of unreality and sensationalism have begun to come to the surface on the pages of that once staid and reliable newspaper.

Following its toadally absurd coverage of the lethal British frog migration, the *Wall Street Journal* reported with, as far as we can tell, a straight face, that the Swiss government had contracted with McDonnell Douglas Corporation to purchase thirty-four F/A-18 Hornet jet fighters for its military arsenal.

"What," astounded readers must be asking, "military arsenal?" I think it's common knowledge that except for the Swiss Army knife (which includes a toothpick and tweezers for god's sake) and a few guys dressed in funny costumes guarding the Vatican, Switzerland has no "military arsenal."

In fact, serious students of history will remember that in 1712 the crowned heads of Europe gathered in Zurich to enter into a pact that granted the Swiss a global monopoly on milk chocolate and yodelling in exchange for renouncing all territorial claims and disbanding its military machine (the so-called "Honda Accord").

My guess, and I hate to say this, is that the *Wall Street Journal*, fearful of competition from other newspapers whose front pages are literally awash in color charts, pie graphs, and opinion polls, is simply making a lot of this stuff up. If this dangerous trend continues, we may soon see the *Wall Street Journal* at grocery store checkout lines featuring banner headlines screaming "Iaccoa Out of Closet! Admits Owning a Chevy" or "Space Aliens From Distant Galaxy Corner Pork Bellies Market" or "Alan Greenspan Confesses: 'I Was Elvis' Love Slave.'"

I don't want to draw any conclusions until my research staff/secretary, Yvonne ("That File's Been Lost for Years") McMillian, has had a chance to check out the Switzerland entry in her children's *World Book Encyclopedia*, but it does appear that the *WSJ* is playing fast and loose with the news in an attempt to hype its sales.

On the other hand, what a dark and grisly business it would be to find out that the reports on Switzerland were true and that while the rest of the nations of the world are busy beating their swords into plowshares, VCRs, and cheap cars, those wonderful folks who gave us perforated cheese and unnumbered bank accounts are secretly arming themselves to the teeth with dreams of territorial expansion. For all we know, General Schwarzkopf may, even now, be girding his considerable loins to repulse a Swiss incursion into neighboring countries—"Operation Dessert Storm."

Today Liechtenstein, tomorrow the world.

July 16, 1991

Lèse-Majesté

According to the honking clamor in the British press last week, one would think that President Bush's recent contretemps with Queen Elizabeth caused a dip in U.S.-British relations approaching the strain which resulted when the Brits torched the White House some years back.

The presidential gaffe took place in London during the summit gathering when President Bush had the temerity to—get this—sit down before Queen Elizabeth at a photo session preceding dinner at Buckingham Palace. The Queen, appropriately aghast, glared at Mr. Bush until he got up, allowed her to take her seat, and then formally requested permission to sit down. Apparently, as a child, Mr. Bush never played "May I."

I was completely sympathetic with the president in that just the week before I had committed a somewhat similar diplomatic blunder while speaking to a group in Bermuda. (I get invited to speak a lot. I don't get reinvited very often, but I am convinced I get invited to speak almost every time a program chairman finds out how much Lewis Grizzard charges for that sort of nonsense.)

The speaking engagement was to a group of eight hundred American lawyers who were holding a meeting in Bermuda (after ruling out Cleveland by a voice vote), and I was informed that the premier, Sir John W. D. Swan, would be sitting at the head table and would make a few remarks prior to my talk.

Those in charge of the affair nervously gathered the head-table party in an anteroom before the banquet was to begin and told us in rigorous detail just how, accompanied by the music of the Bermuda military band, we were to proceed to the head table. It was very much like the lead-in at a high school prom without the spotlight and corsages.

As I was to sit on one side of the podium and Sir John on the other, we were designated as the leaders of our respective sides of the platform and were instructed to march into the ballroom in two lines. I was to lead my line to the right side of and onto the head table and he was to take his to the left.

As we marched from the anteroom to the ballroom, I was suddenly confronted with three ballroom doors and, in a lady-or-the-tiger-like terror, bolted through the far-right door only to run into a sea of people and tables crammed together cheek by jowl. As the music began I sensed it was too late to turn back and I began to lead my nervous little troop through the crush of tables, lifting our haunches over chair backs and making a herky-jerky serpentine path to the right side of the head table.

The premier, a veteran of these affairs, calmly waited with his group in the spacious main center aisle, having understood from the start that we were both to take that path before turning right and left. Somehow, despite the fact that I had to force a path through the densely packed tables, and despite the fact that my wife (behind me in line) was hissing like an asthmatic goose that I was taking the wrong route, I made it to my side of the head table in what I'm sure was record time. My sturdy band of head tablers was half-way up on the stage, where I was being greeted by a good deal of enthusiastic applause from those who assumed I was the premier, when I realized he and his group were still at the starting gate waiting, as it turned out, for my group to show. At that point I did give way to a slight panic and ordered my confused crowd back off the platform until Sir John caught up. We finally came together at the head table and stood while the band blew through the "Star Spangled Banner" and "God Save the Queen" (which, as best I can tell, is a direct rip-off of "My Country 'Tis of Thee," written, I think, by Hogey Carmichael in the 1940s).

It's safe to say that my Marx Brothers maneuver was a breach of protocol and did cause some confusion or, as my wife so sympathetically put it to anyone who would listen following our return to Atlanta, "Rambo here just dorked right out. I mean the premier must have been thinking, 'What a Goofus.'" I was, I confess, a little abashed by the episode and know just how President Bush must have felt, but my victim, the premier, couldn't have been more gracious.

As for the querulous Queen Elizabeth, she should have just been glad that she was dealing with President Bush and not Gerald Ford in the grip of one of his famous Chevy Chase imitations or, worse yet, the old kissing bandit himself, Jimmy Carter, in full presidential pucker.

July 30, 1991

Why Do the Lawyers Quayle and Cower?

Vice President Dan Quayle (who, by all accounts, is very bright, but just doesn't do well on standardized tests) blew into Atlanta last week to speak to the American Bar Association and to visit the Varsity. He got it wrong in both places. He left the Varsity without having eaten a hot dog (though his order of fried onion rings should keep his pelt shining for a week to ten days), and he told the American Bar Association that the United States has too many lawyers, too many lawsuits, and too many excessive damage awards. After hearing Quayle charge that the United States is handicapped in world markets because of its glut of lawyers and lawsuits as compared with less litigious countries like Japan, the lawyers were absolutely beside themselves (which, according to many people, particularly doctors, is their favorite position anyway).

The consternation among the lawyers attending the bar association meeting was widespread, but the pit bulls of the profession, the litigators, seemed to be the most upset, running around with dilated nostrils and foam-flecked withers. Charging Quayle, himself a lawyer, with legal *lèse-majesté*, the battered barristers reacted like Cleopatra, who, having warmed a frozen asp at her bosom, was rewarded when the snake revived and gave her *balcon* a bite. (Many will remember the film version in which Elizabeth Taylor played Cleopatra and Herve Villechaize played the asp.) How sharper than a serpent's tooth indeed!

Apparently the Bush administration is proposing legislation that would require that every time Japan shipped us an automobile, we would retaliate by sending them a lawyer.

Frankly, it was hard for me to get worked up about anything uttered by a vice president who looks like a mystery Cleaver from *Leave It to Beaver: The Missing Episodes*. I think the vice president means well, but he clearly needs to mature some. Washington insiders say that at White House strategy sessions when anyone lights a cigarette, Quayle always begs to blow out the match.

Not only were the lawyers excited about Quayle's inflammatory remarks, my editor was sufficiently bestirred from his customary torpor to call me and suggest I respond to the Quayle calumny. Taking into account that the only calls I usually receive from him are communiqués that my column is running too long and that he and his gnomish and procrustean demi-editors have solved the problem by methodically squeezing the punch lines from each of the gags, I was flattered and flabbergasted.

In any case, I was so enchanted at receiving a phone call from him that I did take another look at Quayle's comments and found they really contained nothing new.

The claim that there are too many lawyers has long been a monotonous theme for an unrelenting and sensationalist press.

As I have said before in this column and from the stump, the notion is sheer nonsense. In point of fact, this country at present has only 550,000 lawyers, more or less, with the result that many people don't even have a lawyer of their own but are forced to share one with someone else. This is not only inefficient but, depending on the particular lawyer involved, downright unsanitary.

Even in the olden days when there were far fewer legal practitioners, there was an unreasoning prejudice against lawyers. The drafters of Georgia's original charter provided that it was to be "a happy, flourishing colony ... free from [as they diplomatically phrased it] the pest and scourge of mankind known as lawyers." Even St. Luke (a known physician) took a gratuitous jab in Chapter 11, Verse 46, with "Woe unto ye lawyers also! For you load men with burdens hard to bear, and you yourselves do not touch the burdens with one of your fingers." He also warned later in the same chapter that it was not wise to draw nigh unto C.P.A.s or state legislators.

My advice to the lawyers is that they should learn to float serenely in this sea of obloquy and should not take themselves or Dan Quayle too seriously. As for Vice President Quayle, I would say, "Get a life. Get a job. Get a chili dog."

August 19, 1991

Eat Lead, Bambi

We may not be winning the battle against drugs or the battle against crime, but after spending a couple of hours driving on Interstate 20 last Sunday, I am absolutely sure we are winning the battle against Bambi.

My son, son-in-law, and I were returning from a round of golf in Augusta and in the space of two hours we must have passed at least one hundred vehicles bearing stone-cold deer carcasses. It was very interesting to observe the rolling aftermath of such a monumental slaughter.

All of the hunters affected some sort of desert storm camouflage outfit, but, in spite of their obvious desire to remain invisible in the woods, most of them also sported orange-colored Day-Glo caps. This might not be as dumb on their part as it would first appear. I suspect it is a psychological gambit which they use to attract the deer. It's easy to imagine a deer saying to his buddy, "Hey, Buck, let's go down that trail over there. You

LEROY MERLE
BUD
JACK DAVIS

won't believe the dork I've spotted in a camouflage suit and orange hat."

All of the hunters were not, as one might imagine, low-browed, hairy-backed males who resemble the characters from the love scene in *Deliverance*. For the most part, except for the paramilitary outfits, they were a pretty ordinary lot, and there were even a few women who apparently joined the carnage on the assumption that "a family who slays together, stays together." (I can just hear the deer-hunter husband now, "Bertha, it gets me *so hot* to see you field-dress a dead buck!")

Their vehicles were big pickup trucks with gun racks in the cab and bumper stickers expressing sentiments like "Nuke the Baby Seals." Almost all of them were bearing a glassy-eyed, tongue-protruding dead deer, some containing as many as four.

High-tech mobility has apparently come to the sport, as many of the trucks were carrying four-wheel motor scooters which are apparently used to track the wily quarry deep into the woods. Some were also carrying little portable seats which, I am told, are somehow placed up in trees to give the hunters yet another advantage in shooting the wary deer. The first advantage, of course, being the fact that the deer themselves are, in most cases, unarmed. Maybe next year the hunters will outfit their pickups with those huge tires so popular with drivers who have the IQ of mildew and mount a 30-caliber machine gun on the cab. With this type rig they could clearly penetrate even deeper into the woods and substantially increase the body count.

After passing an extraordinary number of these meat wagons, my son-in-law said that next Sunday we ought to rent a pickup and make the same run wearing fake deer heads, with one of us lying in the back of the truck in a camouflage suit, glassy-eyed and tongue-protruding. For those who might think his suggestion bizarre, I should point out that he once confessed at a public gathering that his all-time favorite movie was *Caddy Shack*.

All of this causes me to wonder what one would do with a dead deer. I know that in some cultures people actually eat them and I have, in fact, been lured into trying some myself despite fervent protestations that I hate the gamey taste. The standard response is always, "I know, I know, but you haven't tasted it the way *I* cook it." In fact, I've tasted everything from Deer Stroganoff to Stove Top Deer Helper and it all tastes like used sandals to me.

There also exists the wonderful possibility that you can chop off the corpse's head, nail it to a board, and hang it on your wall. Almost all schools of interior design agree that there is nothing like a fur-covered deer skull with marbles in its eye sockets to dress up the old recreation room.

All this sounds like I am some sort of animal-rights nut out to ensure that laboratory rats enjoy their full Constitutional protections. Actually, I don't have anything at all against the deer hunters or the sport itself. After all, it's a lot closer to nature than grown men dressed in loud-colored sweaters and knickers whacking at a ball with a stick. However, I have to confess that when I was looking at all those freshly slaughtered deer last Sunday, I did have a flashback to Oscar Wilde's description of fox hunting. He said it was "the unspeakable in full pursuit of the inedible."

November 13, 1991

Tom Teepen: Forgotten But Not Gone

It's not often that a dilettante columnist like me gets to hang out with real newspaper men (and, of course, newspaper ladies). So one can imagine how excited I was to be in the company of so many of them at the party thrown by the *Atlanta Constitution* for Tom Teepen at one of the city's posh eateries. The Krystal at Northside and Fourteenth Street was the scene of the "Hang the expense, this is for Tom!" gathering, and almost three booths were filled to overflowing with hard-bitten newspaper types wearing cheap suits and snap-brimmed fedoras shouting things like "Stop the press," "Rip out the front page," and "Two chili-pups with cheese!"

Even the toughest of the grizzled news veterans got a little moist in the eye when publisher Jay Smith stood up and, speaking for all of us, said, "At the end of 1991, when the fearless, hard-hitting editorial page editor of the *Atlanta Constitution*, Tom Teepen, steps down (or up, as the case may be) from the post he has held since July 1, 1982, we will truly have come to the end of an error." (We're sure he meant "era".)

I couldn't agree more. Teepen, rumored to be the love child of Grizzly Adams and Bella Abzug (a union which would explain both his appearance and his politics), steps down after eight and a half years as editorial page editor of the *Constitution*. Before that he served for fourteen years in the same post for the *Dayton Daily News* (which in those days was mostly pictures).

In honor of his unyielding, some say "unthinking," liberalism, the prestigious Cobb County Association of Orthopedic Medicine, Video Rentals and Live Bait announced that it was creating the "Tom Teepen Knee Jerk Chair of Liberal Reaction." In addition, the association will install an exhibit in its lobby featuring an actual knee suspended in a clear plastic vat of formaldehyde which will begin to twitch uncontrollably when a viewer utters into an attached microphone certain words like "Bush," "blacks," "baby seals," "Newt," "First Amendment," "Strom," or "big business" (other than big businesses which regularly advertise in the newspapers).

Teepen is truly a man of many parts (which explains, in large measure, why he gets so many laughs in the steam room). Only his closest friends know that he does his own dental work, makes his own clothes (usually ill-fitting double-breasted suits), and owns what is said to be the best collection of nude photographs of Drew Pearson in the country.

As *AJC* editor Ron Martin said at the farewell ceremonies in a voice croaking with emotion (and I think he was speaking for all of us), "Tom Teepen is smarter than he looks."

Throughout the ceremony, Teepen stood like a tower, wearing his trademark ill-fitting double-breasted suit and showing through his hirsute visage a wan smile which, for the most part, resembles a possum lapping syrup out of a live light socket.

At year end, he will join the ranks of so many other former members of the *Constitution* in a journalistic Erebus, suspended, like Mohammed's coffin, between heaven and earth, or, in his case, between the *AJC* editorial offices and Loon Lake. He will be forgotten but not gone.

I think Jay Smith in his concluding remarks at the farewell dinner was speaking for all of us when he said, "Tom Teepen will go down as one of the biggest in the anals of journalism." (We're sure he meant "annals.")

December 14, 1991

There's a Lot of That Going Around

There are sociologists, researchers at large universities, radio talk show hosts, and ultraliberal columnists who are forever squeaking and braying to the effect that there are no gender-based differences when it comes to a person's capacity for compassion in a crisis situation. All this proves to me is that no sociologists, researchers at large universities, radio talk-show hosts, or ultraliberal columnists have ever been attended by my wizened wife during the course of a grisly illness.

The compassion contrast between the genders in my particular case study was made even more pointed by the fact that my own illness was preceded by a minor bout which my wiry wife engaged in with the same malaise.

One Saturday afternoon as I was busy watching professional bowling on television (there would appear to be some sort of league rule that each bowler have no neck and an ugly shirt), I was interrupted by my wife's thin, reedy voice

JACK DAVIS

saying, "I think I'm going to be sick."

As her indisposition had brought her in from an afternoon of cleaning the gutters, I instinctively sensed that it was a serious malady which would require loving care and devoted attention by me. I immediately leaped into action by sitting up on the sofa and suggesting that she should quit cleaning the gutters, put off ironing my shirts until the following day, and go upstairs and take her temperature, saying that as she was going to have to wait around for three or four minutes with a thermometer in her mouth, she might take that opportunity to make me a tuna fish sandwich with sweet pickles and lots of mayonnaise.

At this point her eyes turned completely white, both cheeks extended to their fullest limits, and she bolted from the room with a stricken look.

As soon as possible (I think it was during the halftime ceremonies of a football game I had switched to), I rushed up to our bedroom to attend her, insisting again that she wait until the following day before getting around a hot iron.

I really don't think her episode was quite as severe as mine because in only one day she was, owing to my ministrations and the fact that she lounged around in bed for twenty-four hours, fully restored, an apple-cheeked, chirping picture of health.

Several evenings later, I came home for supper to find her stirring up a large cauldron of low-fat chili which was made from a recipe she found in a book called *The T-Factor Diet.* It allegedly contained only one fat gram per serving and was made with kidney beans soaked in chicken broth, chili powder, and used-truck tire treads which can be found on the side of any interstate highway. Except for the taste and the fact that it had the bouquet of a drag race, you'd have sworn it was the real thing. To her credit, my wizened bride has never been a nag about my weight, but when she learned from my gabby secretary, Yvonne ("Does this letter *have* to go out today?") McMillian, that I had caused my office chair to be let out, she began to bustle around officiously, promoting diets that let you eat "all you want to eat" as long as you eat bean sprouts, yogurt, and plankton flown in daily from Lake Burton.

Although I only ate enough of the chili concoction to show my appreciation, I immediately fell desperately ill (studies at the Center for Communicable Disease have shown that the rankest form of salmonella thrives in a fat-free environment).

I quickly curled up on the main sofa in as close to the fetal position as my girth would allow, covered myself with a gathering of throws, and began to shiver and moan uncontrollably, pausing only for intermittent trips to the lavatory to Speak on the Big White Phone. One would imagine that this would provoke no end of tender attentions and expressions of concern from my spouse of long standing. One could scarcely be more incorrect.

Standing over me with arms akimbo, she declared, "It's that thing I had. There's nothing you can do but tough it out."

Throughout my whole ordeal, she callously refused to administer any medication. This despite the fact that, as a 1/16th Creek Indian, she is in possession of a veritable treasure trove of nostrums involving dried frog viscera, roots, ground berries, and scrapings from the walls of her microwave oven.

While because of my raging fever-induced delirium I cannot be quite sure, I believe I heard her talking on the phone to a friend, and though I was in and out of consciousness, I am reasonably certain I heard her say that I thought I was in a "mordibund" state. This was followed by snorting gales of laughter and what sounded to me like the phrase "a real wussy." As I say, I can't vouch for this last part because of my fevered state, but I gladly offer this incomplete study to any serious researchers who are looking into the compassion gender gap which I am convinced has engulfed our modern society.

If the researchers are not interested in my studies, I'd be more than glad to offer them the rest of the chili.

December 15, 1991

Spin Doctor, Heal Thyself

In the wake of the recent primaries, it is pitiful to see just how befuddled the average man in the street is when it comes to interpreting the results. But that is why the man in the street is still in the street while we wily political pundits are in air-conditioned offices rolling about in Naugahyde swivel chairs shouting things like "Stop the press," "Rip out the front page," and "Where the hell did this marinara sauce on my necktie come from?"

The key to understanding the results of primaries and caucuses (a caucus being the political equivalent of a Tupperware party with ballots) is to understand that the apparent winners are really losers and the apparent losers are really winners. If you will type this on a card and have your spouse pin it on your lapel, it will substantially reduce your confusion and anxiety when reading or hearing about primary or caucus results in the future.

Some of the confusion is understandable in that in the first wave of primaries the media declared Bush, who took 64 percent of the Republican vote in Georgia, 70 percent in Maryland, and 67 percent in Colorado, a loser, while Tsongas "won" in Maryland with 41 percent and Jerry "Beam Me Up" Brown "won" in Colorado with less than 30 percent of the vote.

Senators Harkin and Kerry "won" because, even though their vote counts were lower than Vanna White's IQ, their pictures were in the newspapers several times, giving immense pleasure to their campaign workers and members of their immediate families. Kerry's win was so convincing that his ship of state immediately slipped beneath the surface with a great sucking sound, followed a few days later by the S. S. Harkin. Governor Clinton "won" because no ex-inamoratas staged news conferences that week and, contrary to rumors circulated by Republicans, blood tests confirmed that Mickey Rooney was not his real father.

Pat Buchanan, former media pit bull, "won" because, even though he has about as much chance as Dr. Ruth of winning the Republican nomination, he is sending a "message" to President Bush. It seems to me he could have faxed it in less time and made more money by staying on *Crossfire*, snarling at the liberal who looks like Mr. Peepers about matters of great political moment, while the rest of the universe watches *World Wrestling Federation* and reruns of *Mr. Ed*.

David ("It's Time to Change the Sheets in the White House") Duke "won" because he got a lot of free publicity even though his name wasn't on most ballots, thus giving him a chance to stay in his bunker and work on his upcoming political autobiography, "Just Because You Wear a Pointed Hat Doesn't Mean You Have a Pointed Head."

President Bush "lost" from a public-relations standpoint because, while campaigning in a supermarket, he revealed to the voters that he hadn't been grocery shopping in so long that he was dazzled by bar-code checkouts. This *gaffe* reinforced the widely held view that to Democrats, clipping coupons means cutting those discount things out of the Sunday paper for groceries, while to Republicans, it means tax-exempt bonds.

All of this simply points out the critical importance of reading columnists on the op-ed page of your local newspaper for meaningful interpretations of primary and caucus results except, of course, for those of you who are interested in news on Governor Clinton, which can best be obtained from the papers at the checkout counter of your local supermarket.

March 6, 1992

Cacophony at Chastain

We currently find ourselves in the grip of urban unrest, civil disorder, and borderline anarchy. I'm not referring to the crisis in the inner cities; I'm speaking of the yahoos at Chastain Park who persist in talking and talking and talking throughout the course of the evening concerts there. Those who say that the art of conversation is dying obviously haven't attended a summer concert at Chastain Park recently.

A few evenings back we were the eager guests of our friend Lawyer Ragsdale, who had managed a prime table at Chastain for the Harry Connick Jr. concert. My sinewy spouse of long standing was so enthusiastic at the prospect of seeing and hearing the stud muffin Connick perform that she had volunteered to furnish the entrée for the event. Our taste buds were dazzled by her gourmet meat-loaf-sandwich recipe (take two pieces of white bread, slather with mayonnaise, add meat-loaf—serves one).

Connick took the stage at the designated hour and launched with enthusiasm into his mellow and lively big-band, high-energy performance. But our rapture was incomplete, as the six-some at the table in front of us persisted in their high-decibel conversations on the apparent assumption that Connick had been imported to furnish background music for their gabbing and gorging. One of their number, who was particularly garrulous, punctuated his nonstop talking with occasional explosions of laughter which sounded like a camel coughing up a fur ball.

All this despite the fact that the master of ceremonies had asked everyone to hold down on the talking and Connick himself, at the beginning of his performance (manfully holding his head erect despite the fact that it appeared to be basted with a firkin of styling gel), had pleaded with the crowd not to talk, or, as he said, "If you must talk, then shout at each other so I'll think you're shouting for me."

The chin-music ensemble at the next table was unfazed by all this importuning, chiefly because they were talking relentlessly and heard none of it. The other concertgoers at the tables in our area were, to their credit, as quiet as mice. (They don't call me the "Sultan of Simile" for nothing.)

Midway through the concert, my frustration overcame my reluctance to act like a prissy hall monitor and I leaned over to the braying bunch at the next table and, pointing to Lawyer Ragsdale, said to one of their number, "Pardon me, but this fellow is on a twenty-four-hour furlough from the Georgia State Institute for the Violent and Criminally Insane. This is his only chance to hear a concert this summer and your loud talking is beginning to agitate him some." Happily, my admonition did not fall on entirely deaf ears and for the remainder of the concert our noisy neighbors made some attempt at holding their conversation down to the level of infield chatter at a baseball game. One pretty blonde in their group even turned her chair around and watched the concert for a while.

Emboldened by my small success, I am now assaying the

possibility of writing an insert for the Chastain Park programs which would offer a number of rejoinders, remonstrations, and requests which could be used by other Chastain concertgoers (90 percent of whom, by the way, do not talk during a performance) to subdue their rude and loquacious neighbors. A few early entries are (1) "If the music is interfering with your conversation, perhaps we could ask the band to leave"; (2) "Is there a volume control on your group?"; (3) "Did you know that talking during a concert is a sign of sexual insecurity?"; (4) "Pardon me, I believe your manners are leaking"; (5) "If you don't quiet down, the concert vigilantes are going to kick your butt up around your elbows"; (6) "If you don't can that palaver, you're going to be wearing that candelabra like a pair of antlers"; and (7) "Hey! Shut up!"

It's just one concertgoer's small attempt at addressing a much larger problem, but as the great philosopher Arthur Schopenhauer once said (in an aphorism marvelously apt for Chastain Park concerts), "If everyone lit just one little candle, we'd be up to our asses in hot wax."

June 15, 1992

A Short History of a Small Movement

Younger Lawyers Section Newsletter editor Jim Hyder, confident in the knowledge that old geezer lawyers are easy prey to insincere flattery, sent me a note indicating that the fall 1993 edition of the hard-hitting and world-famous *YLS Newsletter* would feature a "guest speakers column." With the guile and cunning which has typified so many former editors of the *Newsletter* (I'm thinking particularly of Billy Barwick, currently employed with the Snellville firm of Guile & Cunning, where he specializes in witnessing wills and notarizing documents of little import), Hyder suggested that I might inaugurate the series and I am pleased to do so.

The Younger Lawyers Section of the State Bar of Georgia was founded in 1947 in an effort to give younger lawyers something to do with their hands and, in the opinion of many, the section is, next to the Locust Grove Chapter of the United Daughters of the Confederacy, one of the most powerful forces in our state.

Never in history have so many met so often, written so many letters, presented so many plaques to each other, and accomplished so little.

In June of 1963, political observers here and abroad were stunned when the Younger Lawyers Section elected to its highest office a young Lebanese immigrant, Charles J. Driebe or, as he was known to his followers, "Captain Swarthy." (He was also known as the "Father of the *YLS Newsletter*" and was thought to be the love child of an illicit relationship between Omar Sharif and Fanny Brice.) It was Driebe who named me to succeed him as editor in chief of the *Newsletter*, which he had created only a year earlier to promote his candidacy for the president's office. A condition of my being named to head the *Newsletter* was that each subsequent issue had to feature at least six photographs of the incumbent president, Driebe. As an historical aside, it was Driebe who conceived the mass production and distribution of the annual and highly coveted Younger Lawyers Section Award of Achievement, with the result that awards are now given each year to every young lawyer in the state who can dress himself (or in some parts of the state, herself). Many of us thought Driebe was destined for further greatness, but a wave of anti-Arab sentiment in the late '60s and the fact that he moved to Jonesboro, Georgia, caused him to fade into obscurity. He is now head of the Clayton County P.L.O. and is a part-time lookout for a massage parlor on Highway 41 South.

While I was editor of the *Newsletter* it occurred to me that many YLS politicians were taking themselves far too seriously, and I inaugurated a series of biographical sketches (some said "character assassinations") of those sometimes pompous pundits.

Throwing good taste and punctuation to the wind, my biographical sketches extended from August 1963 through 1978, when the silver-tongued, Brilliantine-haired, op-ed editor of the *Atlanta Constitution*, Hal Gulliver, cajoled me into writing a humor column for his newspaper. (Gulliver, for reasons no one can explain, later became a lawyer himself.) Looking back on them I am amazed by my prescient assessment of some of the brighter lights of the YLS Bar. To cite just one example, I go back to January 1973 and quote from the tribute I paid to William Ide, whose investiture as president of the American Bar Association was just completed in New York City in August, 1993.

> In Geneva, Illinois, at precisely 8:26 P.M. on April 23, 1940, while all America was glued to their radios listening to the *Ted Mack Original Amateur Hour* as a frantic unemployed yam grower from Demopolis, Alabama, played "Under the Double Eagle" while clog dancing on an electric whoopee cushion, Roy William Ide III was born to poor but proud parents. The event was to change their lives: while they continued to be poor, they were never proud again.
>
> Ide enjoyed as normal a childhood as was possible for one prematurely bald at age ten. Even this handicap was turned to good advantage, as it led to a full scholarship to Washington & Lee when Ide became the D.A.R. 1957 winner of the Y. A. Tittle Look Alike Contest.
>
> Infuriated by the charge that W&L was a party school, Ide sought out the most challenging courses available, earning a C+ average in folk dancing and shop. Academicians at W&L still recall Ide's brilliant senior thesis, "Over 100 Really Good Knock-Knock Jokes."

This brief sample from the Paleolithic age of the YLS may help to explain why most adult members of the bar consider the *Newsletter* to be a relentless succession of photographs of young lawyers shagging to beach music at some resort obviously not chosen for its conduciveness to continuing legal education. I do remember thinking in 1973 that Ide, because of his relentless aversion to billable time and his uncontrollable passion for attending cocktail parties while wearing a name tag, was bound for greatness in the organized bar. Twenty years later I was proven correct.

I look back in awe to those Younger Lawyers Section giants of yesterday—many of whom are now in nursing homes and detox-ification centers across the state, sitting around with their robes open and muttering to themselves about "special demurrers"—and say to each of them, "Without your dedication and devotion to high purpose, we might not have a Younger Lawyers Section newsletter today." Think about it.

August 11, 1993

You Guys Have Been Great

Anybody watching television lately has to be aware of the fact that there has been a great comedy explosion. Its hapless victims are sitting around in comedy clubs across the nation with tattered senses of humor and funny things hanging off of their clothes. There's scarcely a TV cable channel that doesn't feature stand-up comedy. (According to noted humor experts, sit-down comedy is in the grip of a severe decline and shows no prospect of a resurgence anytime soon.)

Although the comics are, for the most part, entertaining and a few are funnier than Sam Donaldson's hair, I am perpetually mystified by the fact that when their routine is done, they all, to a man (and sometimes to a woman in the case of the softer comics), exit abruptly by saying, "You guys have been great. Good night." This truncated goodbye always leaves me with an empty and unfulfilled sense of *mirthitis interruptus*. One would think that these ultraclever and hip comedians could come up with something a little more original and humorous when they finally run out of comedy rope.

As a public service, I certified this problem to the prestigious Cobb County Institute for Jocundity and Clever Sayings, an institution dedicated to coming up with those hilarious exchanges between TV anchors and their chortling weathermen. They also furnish those side-splitting quips at the end of the articles in *Reader's Digest* and the clever dialogue for fishing shows on cable television ("All right, son! 'At's a big'un!").

In the space of just two days, their staff, located in small but tastefully decorated offices in the Big Chicken, managed to come up with the following offerings, which I pass along to comics at large as new and improved exit lines:

> (1) "My stars, it's nine o'clock (a resourceful comedian will put in the actual time); I've got to go help some friends circumcise their gerbil."
>
> (2) "Well, fun-seekers, I can see by the old comedy dipstick that I've just run out of laughing gas, so, with your permission, I'll just slip offstage and tank up."
>
> (3) "Well, I can tell from the cigarette smoke that it's time for my chest X-ray, so until next time I'll just say 'Hawrk! Hawrk! Hawrk!'" (exit left clutching throat).
>
> (4) "Well, I can tell from the sea of glassy eyes that you guys can't take even one more hilarious comparison about the difference between living in New York and L.A., so I'm outta here!" (The staff at the institute points out that comedians, like young waiters and waitresses, refer to everyone as "guys," regardless of gender.)
>
> (5) "Caramba! I think my bran flakes are about to kick in, so, like the Cisco Kid's sidekick used to say, 'Let's went.'"
>
> (6) "I'll be leaving now, but I'd like to remind you that a standing ovation would impress the club

owner, make me very happy, and give all of you a chance to adjust your underwear."

These are just a few examples of snappy closing lines and, until next time, I just want to say, "You guys have been great. Good night."

November 4, 1993

DRESS FOR SUCCESS

Now that time has put some merciful distance between us and the day-to-harrowing-day agony and ecstasy of the Atlanta Braves' fortunes, we can put on our slippers, ease into the Naugahyde recliner, fill our pipes with some aromatic carcinogen, and reflect on the more meaningful aspects of our great national pastime, baseball.

I can't begin to compete in that connection with deep thinkers like George Will, Roger Kahn, and David Halberstam, whose writings make baseball players seem like mythical figures striding in ten-league boots through roiling seas of statistics to perform some act of cosmic consequence.

My reflections are even shallower than those who sometimes wonder why baseball is so horribly preoccupied with esoteric statistics. ("Well, Skip, if John Kruk scratches himself once more in this inning, he will tie the National League record for the most consecutive displays of bad taste by a first baseman in night games played on natural turf." "Right, Pete, but you know Kruk has a natural advantage in that department. I understand he was the first member of his family to be raised in captivity.")

No, my thoughts are shallower still. While George Will ponders fulsomely on whether baseball and its tidal movements are somehow a metaphor for life and its deeper meanings, I find myself wondering about things like why baseball managers and coaches all wear uniforms just like the players.

As far as I have been able to observe in my monitoring of the sport, there is absolutely no prospect of any of those old geezers actually getting into a game, so I am perpetually puzzled as to why they go to all the trouble of having oversize uniforms cranked out for them to wear. It really isn't likely that Bobby Cox, even with his new wheels, is going to put himself in as a pinch runner or Tommy Lasorda, the Ultra-Slim Fast dropout, will waddle in to pinch hit.

This phenomenon is made all the more curious by the fact that coaches in all other sports wear regular clothes during a game. Well, in the case of Jerry Glanville, the clothes are not all that "regular." In full plumage he looks like the Durango Kid on steroids, and if that belt buckle gets any bigger, he's going to give himself a vasectomy if he sits down too quickly.

Baseball managers and coaches don't have to wear costumes that match those of their players. The legendary manager, Connie Mack, managed to manage very well in a three-piece suit with high-top lace-up shoes and a derby hat. However, baseball historians suggest that one of the reasons he was reluctant to wear a pair of baggy flannel knickers and a billed beanie was that he was already self-conscious about having a girl's name.

I think there should be a call for consistency in the world of professional sports and if we can't talk Lasorda, Mazzone, et al., into street clothes during a ball game, maybe a rule ought to be passed requiring coaches and managers in other sports to dress up like their players. Perhaps the Atlanta Knights could break the ice (so to speak) by having their coach show up in one of those padded cells that hockey players zip around in. I'm sure Pat Riley would look just fine in a singlet, shorts, and knee pads assuming he could get a release from *GQ*.

There are a lot of things that are beyond our control, but we can, at least, seek some symmetry in sports. As that great American philosopher Ralph Waldo Fregosi once said, "Clothes make the man but not the manager." Let George Will ponder on that.

December 15, 1993

Sinewy Spouse Redux

I was striding briskly through Central City Park recently when a complete stranger accosted me. (In Georgia strangers are required by law to be "complete," "total," or "perfect." There have been no confirmed sightings of a perfect stranger in Atlanta since 1946, when one was seen leaving the old Frances Virginia Tea Room.)

The man fixed me with a baleful gaze and said, "You haven't written anything about your 'sinewy spouse' in a long time. Are you two still married, and is she still saying those weird things?" Despite my ringing assurance that my wiry wife of long standing and I were still in a state of wedded bliss, the gimlet-eyed fellow continued his suspicious line of inquiry, hinting obliquely that if word of my desiccated helpmate didn't surface in a column soon, he might urge law-enforcement agencies to begin digging up my patio. His gratuitous prompting causes me to affirm publicly that our union, like a chronic sinus condition (never fatal, always painful), is now in its thirty-fifth year, and she is, indeed, still spouting those "weird things" with the relentlessness of tracer bullets.

Although she is a college graduate and can name the capitals of many states (particularly those in the southeast which border Georgia), is a very talented painter, and is an honor graduate of the Imelda Marcos School of Serious Shopping (the woman *has* some shoes), for some quirky reason she has an extraordinary capacity for bizarre utterance. I think her dyslexic locution could be caused by (1) some chemical imbalance resulting from years of drinking iced tea so sweet that it would make Willie Wonka pucker in revulsion, (2) attempting conversations with house pets, or (3) some twisted circuitry in her brain caused by years of fricasseeing her medulla oblongata as she leans into a wall-rattling, gale-force hair dryer. Whatever the reason, she speaks like someone from another galaxy.

Some of her utterances are technically correct but just about thirty degrees off course, as in the compliment she paid to an elderly friend on seeing her home, "I love this house; every niche has its own special place." Or, in rendering a sports assessment, "Those Falcons are in a low slump." Or, when telling a friend about our recent vacation, "Istanbul was great. It was everything we never expected." Or, when assessing someone's bland personality, "You could not discern his demeanor." Or, when describing a friend racing to answer an urgent call of nature, "She was going up those stairs like a salmon when it goes lemming."

Often she will simply mangle a word or phrase, as in "I think Randy Travis just egludes essence." Or, "I was just prouncing around New York." Or, "He's got a whole new leash on life." Or, "It's a mute question." Or, "I don't squelch on my bets." Or, "He was very suspicious . . . looking very furgative." Or, "He is very unsophisticated. He seems almost like a clout." Or, "That Richard Gere jingles my jibes."

Sometimes she will make a declarative statement that would

give a hernia to an English teacher challenged to diagram it, as in her recent vigorous anticrime pronouncement that, "All police say that a deterrent, no matter what kind, is a dog." This verbal dropping so strained the capacity of our friend Allison, who made a foolhardy attempt to parse it mentally, that he was forced to sit down and fan himself vigorously for several minutes.

Other times, she will give a response that is grammatically correct but dreadfully off-center. She was recently showing a dinner guest of ours a painting that she had done of a former housekeeper and baby-sitter who was very dear to us. She extolled the grand qualities of the good woman so enthusiastically that the guest finally asked, "Is she dead?" to which my wife replied, "No, but she can't be reached by phone." The effect of such a response on a normal person is hard to describe.

I've found through bitter experience that it never pays to inquire into the deeper meaning of her sayings. Witness the following colloquy:

She: "He was looking kind of innoculous."

Me: "What is 'innoculous'?"

She: "It means he was having thoughts about nothing."

These exchanges cause a sharp pain behind my eyes, and I have learned to avoid them at all costs.

But, yes, complete stranger, we're still married, and strange as it may seem, her weird speech warp seems to eglude essence and never fails to make my jibes jingle.

February 2, 1994

One of a Kind

My old friend and boon golfing companion, Lewis Grizzard, the "Muse of Moreland," holed out on Sunday, March 20, 1994. A field marshall in the war on solemnity and against the ever-swelling ranks of the humor impaired has laid down his baton.

I was pleased to have had a long visit in the hospital with him only a few days before his death, attended his eleventh-hour nuptials, a rousing, lively and therapeutic wake presided over by his physician and friend, Randy Martin, and, finally, the memorial services at the Moreland Methodist Church. All of these activities, while offering some balm to the premature loss shared by so many, still fell short of closing the chapter on our friendship.

Like all who came in contact with Lewis, I was a victim of "friend abuse" at his hands. When someone made so bold as to publish a collection of my columns under the title *The Sass Menagerie*, Lewis offered a jugular-slicing blurb that read, "With

CLOUD NINE
JACK DAVIS

this book Bob Steed has done for literature what Jimmy Swaggart has done for cheap motels." On an earlier dubious literary enterprise of mine titled *Money, Power and Sex (A Self-Help Guide for All Ages)*, Lewis coughed up the following harumph for the dust jacket—"Bob Steed knows as much about money, power and sex as Boy George knows about testosterone."

However, Lewis could take it as well as give it, and he never seemed to hold it against me when I introduced him at various speaking engagements over the years by saying, "I am always amazed at Lewis Grizzard. I'm primarily amazed because he is one of the few University of Georgia graduates I know who can write sentence after sentence . . . many of them containing both a noun and a verb." It used to always confound Georgia Tech graduates when I told them that "Go Dawgs" *is* a complete sentence. And, before I get a lot of mail (in crayon) from University of Georgia graduates saying what a towering citadel of scholarship it is, I want to say in advance that I had two daughters who graduated from that institution and both of them, while in attendance, took roller skating for credit.

Lewis also seemed to appreciate the research I engaged in after his first pig valve implant as to what happened to his old heart valve. I learned from some doctors at Emory that Lewis's valve had been placed in the pig's heart and that the pig underwent a severe personality change. He began wearing little Gucci loafers and glasses, grew a mustache, and wound up writing a newspaper column under the name of Ron Hudspeth.

Before the memorial service one of our mutual friends came up to me and said, "Now that Lewis is gone, you're going to have to write more often." It was a happy thought and I was flattered to hear it expressed, but the chasm left in the 450 newspapers from sea to shining sea that published Lewis's columns is too wide and deep for anyone else to ever fill. Lewis was one of a kind. To borrow a phrase from another humor writer of some renown, the late S. J. Perelman, "They broke the mold before they made Lewis Grizzard."

During the funeral services for Lewis, my mind began wandering back to happier times of golf outings together in Atlanta, Newnan, Augusta (his first outing at Augusta National), Ireland, and Scotland (during my last hospital visit, we talked about mounting a golfing expedition to Spain), and the happy memories began the healing process of pushing aside the somber ones. I even found myself dreaming up typical titles for Grizzard books. The last one flashed across my mind's eye as the Moreland Methodist choir was winding up on "Precious Memories."

It went, "If Heaven Ain't a Lot Like Ansley Golf Club, Then I Don't Want to Go."

Lewis, we'll miss you. Keep hitting 'em straight.

March 25, 1994

Learn to Live with It

For those of you who don't keep up with the obscure but, I'm sure, profitable celebratory events dreamed up by brainstorming executives of the greeting-card industry, this is National Secretaries Week. ("Listen to this, chief, what about 'National Crossing Guards Day' or maybe a week honoring your neighborhood proctologist, like, 'When the hospital gown starts to fall, I keep my back against the wall.'")

How, you may ask, do I know that this week is National Secretaries Week? The answer is simple. My trusted and efficient secretary of long standing, Yvonne ("That file's been lost for years") McMillian, never fails to give me advance and pointed notice followed by fulsome particulars on how other bosses are planning to honor their secretaries with lunches, gifts, cash bonuses, days off, etc.

This year was no exception as Yvonne ("Does this letter really have to go out today?") McMillian issued the annual alert she has been giving me since she signed on as a sassy, red-haired eighteen-year-old in 1963.

As she stood there expectantly, obviously willing to interrupt her morning marathon of nail buffing and personal phone calls to make reservations at an expensive restaurant, I began to wax nostalgic about her thirty-plus-year span of secretarial service.

She came to our chambers fresh from the prestigious Marsh Business School (whose seal bore the Latin phrase *carpe maxim*—"Let them get their own damn coffee"), where she excelled at long lunch hours and talking back.

I vividly remember calling one of her references, a secretarial sciences teacher at South Cobb High, who seemed excessive in her praise of Yvonne's personality. It turned out to our dismay after Yvonne was hired that "good personality" was a code phrase for "She can't type a lick."

She was assigned to me and Lawyer Hurst, who was my senior, and we loaded her down with a mountain of accumulated work. The spunky young employee worked for eight hours straight and then turned in her resignation. Lawyer Hurst, in a spasm of avuncular advice, told her that she would regret such a decision for the rest of her life and convinced her to stay. She never forgave him.

However, she learned to type up a storm and mastered all the other secretarial skills, such as taking the blame for her bosses' errors, lying on the phone as to his availability or whereabouts, doing his children's tax returns, performing all manner of personal errands his wife assumed he was doing, etc., etc.

My eyes brimmed as I suddenly became aware of all she had done for me over those three decades, and in a spontaneous but uncharacteristic outburst, I blurted, "Miz Mac, what would you do if I told you that you were responsible for what I am today?" Fixing me with a baleful stare she replied, "I guess I'd just have to learn to live with it."

Yvonne, from me and all the gang at Hallmark ("For those who care enough to buy a card rather than thinking up their own greetings"), Happy National Secretaries Week.

April 27, 1994

My God, They're Back!

Some would think that after Jimmy Swaggart committed his clerical error and Jim Bakker (the extra "k" was for "kash") had his zip code changed by law-enforcement authorities, the God-cable channel airways would be free for a while of those God-praising, fund-raising, tub-thumping, Bible-slapping, suck-back, electronic-plate-passing televangelists. However, in doing some channel surfing over a recent weekend, I stumbled across a "Praise-a-Thon" in full cry on Atlanta Cable's Channel 26, the Trinity Broadcasting Network, and it provoked some flash-backs to those holy halcyon days when Jim and Tammy Faye Bakker were hooting and hollering to raise money for what was going to be the largest water slide in Christendom near Fort Mill, South Carolina.

The organizers of the Praise-a-Thon were beaming their sup-plications from sea to shining sea, with the United States divid-ed, like Gaul (or, in this case, gall) into three parts, and, in an enterprising bit of mendicancy, were having each section compete against the other two to see which could bring in the most sheaves. Most of the time the program was presented in triple split screen, with all three studios engaging in holy high jinks, challenging the laggard sections of the United States to catch up with the front running section.

The Praise-a-Thon featured a lady MC who looked eerily like the ever-lachrymose Tammy Faye. She had the basket-size blonde hairdo, the eye makeup which caused her to look like she had gone over the wall at The Betty Ford Center for Maybelline Abuse and, while she didn't burst into tears as much as Tammy Faye, she could sniffle convincingly enough when the spirit moved her.

She was running her part of the show from a studio in Houston, Texas, but, if I understood matters correctly, was married to an elderly silver-haired (and -tongued) fellow in the California studio who wore western outfits that would make Porter Waggoner twitch in unrestrained envy. Beyond that, she was happy to the point of hysteria and laughed at all of her own utterances with a giddiness that made me think nitrous oxide was being pumped into the air-conditioning system.

There was a lot of tambourine banging and song singing about bouncing around in Beulah Land, going to the Hallelujah Shore, and tears which would never stain the streets of that City. All of this musical carrying on made me recall an old and apt gospel favorite of my own titled, "Everybody Talking 'Bout Heaven Ain't Going There."

The Tammy Faye look-alike said, "Some of you are hearing ten thousand dollars. Some of you are hearing fifty thousand dollars. It's not the devil talking to you. The devil doesn't talk to you about giving to TBN. Some of you are hearing one hundred thousand dollars." I was hearing a ringing noise as she went on to discuss healing, winding up with a story about having seen a chicken healed when she was a young girl. I'm assuming there are reduced rates for healing poultry, but she was never specific on that point.

However, before any scoffers begin scoffing, they should know that at one point during the Praise-a-Thon, the tote board registered in excess of sixty million (that's right, million) dollars raised in that particular effort. While it was never clear during the several hours I watched the show as to what the millions of dollars were going to be applied, my guess is that based on the gaudiness of the studio sets, much of it will be used to gild every stick of furniture in the Western world. The Praise-a-Thon sets are never going to make it into *Architectural Digest*. We're talking serious bad taste, white grand pianos and gold-covered everything. Imagine a tent revival being held in Pano and Paul's.

I don't want to draw any conclusions until I have seen a lot more of this enterprise, but I am happy to report that I will be keeping an Argus eye out to see if we have yet another wave of adherents to the biblical admonition first espoused in Deuteronomy (I think), where the Old Testament prophet, Ralph (I think) said, "If you are going to abide the flock, you might as well shear the sheep."

Stay tuned.

June 8, 1994

This Corral Isn't O.K. with Me

I've always thought it would be a good job to be a movie critic. Your employer gives you money to go to the picture show, you don't have to wear a necktie, and the workplace is cool and dark.

However, I could never get the job, because if a movie is pathetic from the start, my type-A personality causes me to get out of the theater much in the manner of a mail bag leaving a rail siding. The much-ballyhooed *Wyatt Earp*, an overstuffed, underexposed, self-important, cliché-ridden oat-burner, provoked just such an early exit recently.

From the start it seemed that the folks who made the movie decided to see just how long they could drag out every scene, and the opening segment—teenage Wyatt Earp running through a panoramic sea of corn while pursued by his daddy, the gruff but lovable Gene Hackman—caused me to begin fidgeting uncontrollably.

The filmmakers then telegraphed that this was an "epic" by

DODGE
Z
Z
O.K.
CORAL
JACK DAVIS

ending every scene with a swollen crescendo of *Doctor Zhivago*-type symphony music. This annoying device was pursued with such relentless vigor that it finally became an unintentionally comic moment, punctuating the end of every scene.

Teenage Earp ultimately grows up to be Kevin Costner who drifts through this vehicle like a victim of early narcolepsy. It could be that young Earp had a frontier lobotomy before the opening credits began to roll, but no mention was made of any such procedure even though excessive attention was paid to much less interesting biographical detail. Hackman, to his credit, simply looked embarrassed when he was on screen.

Moviegoers have learned through eye-straining years of squinting that movies "filled with meaning" are dark movies, and the makers of *Wyatt Earp* reinforce its importance by apparently having filmed it through the windows of one of those pimpmobiles you see cruising around town.

The movie was a veritable cavalcade of silver screen clichés. Among them, one showed the moony-eyed Costner doing a poor imitation of Jimmy Stewart as he goes through a tediously naive wooing segment in which he charms and wins his wife. Another cliché has the now dewy-eyed Costner being brought to his knees by the loss of his wife (who, happily for her future as an actress, dies of typhoid early in the movie). This causes Costner's emotions to run the gamut from A to B and instantly turns him into a drunken lout who, in a fit of black rage, burns their cute little bungalow, becomes the cowboy equivalent of a street person, ultimately steals a horse, and winds up in jail to confront the grim visage of Hackman, who arrives with bail money and portentous advice which Costner should have taken literally—get out of town. At this point in the movie, I was busy holding up Jujy Fruits to what little light was available trying to be sure that I didn't accidentally eat a licorice-flavored one.

The clichés began to pop up even faster during the disgustingly memorable buffalo-skinning segment. Here they even repeat the old chestnut about the hero ordering a nonalcoholic beverage at a rough western bar (though the director does make a pass at originality by having Costner order coffee instead of sarsaparilla), with the inevitable scoffing by the tough drunk, the predictable backing down of the tough drunk by the hero, etc., etc., etc. Again, *Victory at Sea* orchestra music brings the tiresome segment to a close.

The last cliché I was able to stomach deals with Wyatt Earp, now a hard-bitten sheriff, marshall, meter-maid, whatever, in Dodge City, who is getting on everyone's very last nerve with his ruthlessly efficient police work. (Picture Elliott Ness in chaps.) Two of his newly badged buddies are trying to reason peaceably a couple of yahoos into giving up their gun belts as required by local ordinance when, without any sort of Miranda warning, Wyatt Earp comes up and brains the gun bearing louts with his pistol. While his friends remonstrate with him about police brutality, Wyatt verifies his sixth sense by smugly pulling a derringer from the sleeve of one of the galoots.

At this point in the opus, filled with an overwhelming sensation that it would only be a matter of time before someone would say to Wyatt, "It's quiet down there," and he would reply, "Yes, too quiet," I woke my sinewy spouse, who by that time was about as somnolent as Costner, and got the hell out of Dodge.

I sincerely hope, for the sake of those easily entertained souls we left behind, that the inevitable *Götterdämmerung* in the O. K. Corral was worth the wait, but for me the movie should be retitled *Wyatt Twerp*, quietly withdrawn by the studio and promptly cut into mandolin picks. Two thumbs down.

July 11, 1994

Standing in the Need of Piths

During the course of the recent political unpleasantness I was struck by just how often officeholders and officeholder wannabes would serve up bits of folk wisdom allegedly learned at the knee of their mother/father/grandparent/professor/family proctologist, etc.

The campaign seemed to be marked by a sustained spasm of self-serving shibboleth spouting such as, "My grandmother always told me an incumbent should never agree to a debate with an underdog." Or, "As my late Daddy used to say, 'An incumbent's tax returns are nobody else's damn business.'" If the relative proffering the helpful bromide was both dead and of some ethnic persuasion, it seemed to invest the quote with even deeper meaning, as in, "I don't care what the press thinks, the girl said she was eighteen and, like my late Armenian grandmother used to say, 'The dogs bark but the caravan moves on.'" (Politicians will often end a sentence with both a preposition and a cliché.)

Over the course of the campaign I became grimly aware of the fact that my parents, grandparents, et al., had been dismally derelict in failing to pass along to me any wise and apt aphorisms with which I could pepper my conversation and pass on to my progeny.

In dredging back over a lifetime of memories, I could only recall one tidbit imparted by my late father. In 1954 as he was putting me on a Greyhound bus bound from Bowdon, Georgia, to Macon and my first year of college, he looked me square in the eye, grasped my arm with his big calloused hand and said, "Don't let those folks at Mercer make you room with anyone who wears them brief-type jockey shorts." I never fully understood what he meant by that advice, but it's been a code I've always tried to live by.

In any case, I felt my inventory of sage sayings woefully barren and bereft of bromides. Even more sobering was the realization that I had no database of meaningful maxims to pass along to my own children, who doubtless have been pecking through my conversational droppings for years in search of some illuminating kernels of wisdom.

This bleak thought was so troubling that I resolved to remedy the situation and, setting my chin as firmly as my ample wattles would permit, I racked my mind and memory for pithy epigrams to pass along to my eager offspring. My exertions were rewarded, and after only a few days I had already begun to compile a worthy repertoire.

I see myself in a cardigan sweater and slippers smoking a pipe full of Taster's Choice while sitting before a knot of rapt grandchildren and sharing a few of the following wisdom-encrusted gems:

(1) Unless you *want* to smell like the Gabor sisters, avoid shaking hands with men who wear those musk-laden colognes.

(2) Don't stand near a microwave oven if you're wearing a truss.

(3) Never pick up a hitchhiker wearing nothing but a cowboy hat and a hospital gown.

(4) Nobody's life is completely worthless. You can always serve as a bad example.

This is, admittedly, just a small beginning, but, as my late Latvian great-grandmother used to say, "Bubba, Disneyworld wasn't built in a day."

January 23, 1995

INFOMERCIALMANIA

No sooner than Speaker Gingrich came down from Mount Kennesaw bearing stone tablets graven with the Contract with America did there arise a cry from every nook and cranny (not to be confused with a small Marietta law firm by the same name) clamoring for changes to the Contract. Like the old gospel song "Everybody Wants to Go to Heaven But Nobody Wants to Die," the righteous and politically aware are eager for reform so long as it doesn't empty any trough from which they have been furiously feeding.

Indeed, I, myself, began to think up pressing issues which Representative Gingrich's Contract does not encompass, and fretted intermittently as to whether some of my concerns weren't matters of more cosmic consequence than term limits, balanced budgets, and the sheer unsightliness of Alfonse D'Amato.

Specifically, I think Congress should immediately launch

SHELLACK
Hi MOM!
LENO
LETTERMAN
REVARO
RUSH
CRACKER JACK
TV TICKET
NBC GOODY BAG
TODAY
TV TICKET
TV TICKET
TV TICKET
ABC
OPRA
TV TICKETS
TV TICKETS
JACK DAVIS

hearings on those studio audiences who show up for television infomercials and determine what laws can be passed to keep members of those audiences from getting married and reproducing or, worse yet, getting licenses to operate heavy machinery and equipment on public thoroughfares.

A number of serious questions need to be addressed in this regard, such as: (1) Where do they dredge up those folks who appear in infomercial audiences? Are they paid? Are they given any mind-altering drugs which might explain their hand-clapping, foot-stomping enthusiasm for miracle cleaners, cookware, space-age mops, etc.? (2) Is there any connection between someone who would serve as a studio audience member for an infomercial and those pitiful tourists who wander around in stretch pants and running shoes, carrying their valuables in what looks like a canvas colostomy bag strapped to their waists?

The producers of the infomercials are obviously doing something to whip the studio infomercial audiences into a state which ultimately causes foam to fleck their withers. I speculate that if the collective applause reaches a certain volume level, handlers come out of the wings and throw bits of fish or beef jerky to the audience. The crowds who sign up for the infomercials I have seen look like they would turn up for a root canal if it involved free tickets and snacks of some sort. Can't you hear the dialogue now: "No, you have to write in earlier for tickets to the Letterman show. However, we do have some good seats left for an infomercial in which a glabrous goober volunteers from the audience to come onstage and have his bald spot spray-painted with an aerosol can." (That there are grown Americans who will volunteer to appear on television having their skulls shellacked is continuing proof that cousins really shouldn't marry.)

I've noticed that infomercials seem to employ people from England as hucksters with great frequency, operating on the theory that an English accent—even a cockney one—adds credibility to the pitch. There is a dwarfish cockney redhead who is featured on a number of them and he begins each sentence with the name of the doofus moderator—"Mike, we brought this car in from the junk yard, and, Mike, would you believe we could get such a professional shine on it?" At the end of the infomercial Mike and the dwarf start teasing the crowd about how much they are going to give away for just $39.95. Not just one plastic bottle of car wax which would regularly sell for $19.95, but *two* more plastic bottles of car wax *plus* a buffing rag (retail value $12.95) and a year's supply of car floss. Each time they add another piece of dreck merchandise to the pile, the infomercial studio audience goes berserk with a combination of glee, amazement, hysteria, and thunderous applause.

An extraordinarily high percentage of infomercials seem to involve the peddling of skin or hair products. Aging starlet Victoria Principal seems to be on every other channel flogging some eponymous unguents so extraordinary they require thirty minutes of sustained talking to explain. The poor woman has a concern with moist skin which borders on the obsessive.

In the hair category, the most recent infomercial flooding the airwaves are those that have to do with hanging little pieces of fake hair in a woman's regular hair to fluff up her do. They had these same things when I was in high school, but they never caught on because of an unfortunate marketing decision to call them "rats." Now, nothing seems to light up an infomercial studio audience more than some self-satisfied huckster pulling eight or ten rats out of an old lady's hair.

As my wife (the leathery language butcher) said when summing up a particularly bad movie (it was Robert Altman's *Ready to Wear* for those of you who still have a chance to avoid it), "I've got just two words for all that—'In ane.'"

March 10, 1995

Pornographic Memory

Recognizing fully that nostalgia, like incontinence, is an affliction of old age, I must nonetheless confess to experiencing a wave of it (nostalgia, not incontinence) when I noted in the recent obituaries that the 1950s TV personality Jerry Lester had been permanently cancelled.

I subscribe to S. J. Perelman's practice of getting up and turning immediately to the obituaries and, if I find I'm not included, planning the rest of my day. I was thus engaged some weeks past when I saw in the newspaper's roll call of the recently expired a short obituary chronicling the death of Jerry Lester at age 85.

My fading memory swept me back to the early days of television and the *Broadway Open House*, a vaudeville-style mixture of music and jokes which ran on NBC in 1950 and 1951 and which was hosted by Jerry Lester. It is generally conceded to be the precursor of all network late-night shows.

Lester was a typical Borscht Belt comedian who shared co-hosting duties of the *Broadway Open House* with Morey Amsterdam, later to gain fame as a player on the *Dick Van Dyke Show*. Lester's overblown style involved gags delivered from the side of his mouth followed by rim shots from the drummer. He was an absolute master of eyebrow innuendo and, in that regard, while I remember Lester and Amsterdam vividly, the performer from the *Broadway Open House* who is etched most vividly in my memory is a *zaftig* blonde named Dagmar. (I am blessed with what doctors characterize as a "pornographic memory.") The stupefyingly constructed Dagmar achieved one-name fame long before Cher, Elvis, Madonna, or Kato.

In 1949, my father went deep into debt to buy one of the first television sets in Bowden, Georgia, conferring instant celebrity status upon our family. It was an RCA cabinet model (with doors) which, at $450, had a higher value than all of the rest of our furniture put together. Neighbors would begin dropping in around 9:00 A.M. to watch the WSB-TV test pattern and, in good weather conditions, exclaim about its clarity. Programming was very limited, but the *Broadway Open House* was a definite 11:00 P.M. high point for me as Dagmar, in gowns so low that you couldn't tell if she was in them and trying to get out or out of them and trying to get back in, never failed to provoke adolescent spasms of heavy breathing and impure thought. She played the quintessential dumb blonde, and her skirts were tight to the point that her short steps caused her to walk like an American tourist after a bad Mexican meal.

The marvelously voluptuous Dagmar had been signed on by Lester to deliver recitals of inane poetry in a wonderfully ingenuous, deadpan manner. The poems were a secondary attraction to her bountiful *balcon* and ultimately she stole so many scenes from Lester that he abandoned the series for greener pastures (or less competitive *tetons*).

For hard-core nostalgia buffs, other ministars on the show

included the Mellow Larks, the Honey Dreamers, and the eponymous Milton DeLugg Quartet, featuring the accordion player, Milton DeLugg.

The banter between DeLugg and Lester was a precursor to the now ritualistic discourse which followed between Johnny Carson and Doc Sevrensen, David Letterman and Paul Schaffer, and Jay Leno and Branford Marsalis.

It's hard to imagine that all of these vivid black-and-white memories go back forty-five years, and that somber realization evokes the lines written in the movie *Network* by Patty Chayevsky for William Holden to the effect that "One morning you wake up and realize for the first time that it's a hell of a lot closer to the end than it is to the beginning."

Indulging in nostalgia does indeed provoke the grim realization that the shadows are growing longer or, as that great American philosopher Ralph Waldo Emerson (it was either Ralph Waldo Emerson or Pigmeat Markham; I always get those two mixed up), so succinctly put it, "*Tempus* sho do *fugit.*"

Robert L. Steed
April 21, 1995